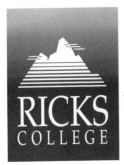

Reinterpretations of Elizabethan Drama

Selected Papers from the English Institute

D# 119209

REINTERPRETATIONS OF

ELIZABETHAN DRAMA

 EDITED WITH A FOREWORD

BY NORMAN RABKIN

Columbia University Press · *New York and London* · *1969*

FOREWORD

WERE THE STUFF of intellectual history a more orderly business, if it could be encapsulated in a rubric like "progress" or examined like the terms of a syllogism or the steps in an argument, if we could watch over the steady march of the years the regular changes in points of view and modifications of approach, then we could easily predict the responses to a topic like "Reinterpretations of Elizabethan Drama" when the English Institute asks for essays that encompass it. But in literary criticism as in everything else the mind produces no such patterns. Rather it achieves periods of stability that rest on the assumptions of a cultural moment; and then, in times of convulsion in which the old assumptions are tossed about so that sometimes they are invisible beneath the waves while at others they are all that is visible on the crest, new ways of seeing come into being that were literally unimaginable to earlier generations.

The pattern in the history of criticism—or of theatergoing—thus resembles the pattern of scientific progress described by Thomas S. Kuhn in *The Structure of Scientific Revolutions.* What men can see in the world in a particular period is dictated by a "paradigm," a schematic ordering of the perceived field which seems for the moment to do away with anomalies. Kuhn demonstrates that the history of science is a record not of gradual accretion and improvement, but rather of a cyclical pattern in which a governing paradigm, first widely accepted as the basis of truth in a given area, then stretched to accommodate anomalies that otherwise might threaten its dominance, suddenly gives way to a new paradigm which grows rather from the anomalies than from the established scheme. The transformation of vision is as revolutionary, Kuhn argues, as the literal transformation of vision afforded to a man who, having learned to see the world through inverting lenses, removes his glasses and sees a new world. "Something like a paradigm is prerequisite to perception itself," Kuhn suggests, and the paradigm is therefore so central to perception that "the proponents of competing paradigms practice their trades in different worlds."

A prototype of Kuhn's radical formulation has long been commonplace as an assumption of literary criticism: the notion that what men see is made possible and limited by the perspective from which they see is a basis for the analysis of character in fiction and a justification for the study of poets' biographies. But Kuhn's formulation so crystallizes that assumption that it is itself a new paradigm, providing a point of view from which one might fruitfully reassess the history of literary criticism. One might observe, for example, how moralistic assumptions about the nature and function of literature entertained in the Enlightenment, themselves a paradigmatic simplification derived from one aspect of Renaissance critical theory—the praise of poetry as instructor—became at the last overcodified, overdefensive in the mode of all paradigms that have outlived their value. The unquestioned assumption that Shakespeare as greatest poet must also be the greatest moralist led naturally and inevitably to the rewriting of his plays so that they would conform to what men with their heads screwed on right could see they added up to. But as the paradigm came too clearly to demand that the world it comprehended must strain to accommodate it, doing away with the paradigm and finding a new one ultimately became a more comfortable process, with the result that even before the full bloom of romanticism it was the gothic, the barbarous, the sublime in Shakespeare rather than his moral wisdom that came to be the mark by which one recognized his work as authentic.

I am quite certain that every contributor to this volume would be horrified to have his essay presented as part of a manifesto. As a matter of fact, much of what the writers do is perfectly traditional, and their essays, uniformly quiet in tone, are addressed to an audience which will almost certainly not be shocked by much of what they say. Nevertheless, taken as a whole this volume reflects a marked shift in approach, indicating the emergence of a new paradigm for the study of Renaissance drama if not of all theatrical art. The essays are not clarion calls to revolution. They do not announce for the first time a radical solution to problems that have beset earlier generations. Rather they embody assumptions which the reader will recognize as shared with much of the most interesting work going on in the criticism of the arts at the present moment. The writers would certainly not agree on all matters of interpretation, or even on the value perhaps of each other's essays. Yet all of them discuss the play as earlier critics neither could nor wanted to: the play as it impinges on its audience, as it is experienced.

Such discussion requires a new assessment of the relation between the work of art and the subjective experience, a new understanding of the interaction between the play and the mind. Ultimately one assumes it demands a full psychological account

of the viewer himself, but strikingly the authors share an interest
above all in the object itself as the means to that account, and do
not attempt what may in fact not be possible to achieve. Agreeing that their concern with a play is to a great extent a concern
with its audience, they seem to agree also that the new concern is
best served by a new kind of scrutiny of the play itself. In the
view which I believe they hold in common of the work of art as
a complex and highly determined shaping of an audience's responses, the writers are freed from the increasingly deadening
obligation to an old paradigm to reduce works to meanings,
though in varying degrees all the authors obviously retain a vital
interest in "meaning" as part of what they examine, or to view
the work of art as a self-enclosed thing in itself. Their new freedom allows them to chart new directions in the understanding of
art which earlier generations once seemed fully to have explored,
while participating in a community of new thinking which is
just beginning to be aware of itself. The implicit and explicit
concern with the role of the audience reveals the intellectual kin-
ship of the essays in this volume with other recent work in which
the new paradigm has begun to emerge: E. H. Gombrich's *Art
and Illusion*, Rudolph Arnheim's *Art and Visual Perception*,
Leonard B. Meyer's *Emotion and Meaning in Music* and *Music,
the Arts, and Ideas*, Morse Peckham's *Man's Rage for Chaos:
Biology, Behavior, and the Arts*, Barbara H. Smith's *Poetic Clo-
sure: A Study of How Poems End*, and Stanley Fish's *Surpris'd
by Sin: The Reader in Paradise Lost*.

It is an interesting paradox that the concern with the responses of the audience entails no less concern than before, perhaps more in fact, with the play itself. As with the scientific

paradigms described by Kuhn, brought into being by the resistance of the world to established and ossified schemata, what I have been calling a new paradigm is obviously a response to the continuing reluctance of Renaissance plays to fit into the systems we have built for them in the past. What can be discerned as new in the approaches of the critics represented here arises from an intense concern with the plays of Shakespeare and his contemporaries, and a recognition of the degree to which other ways of seeing them have distorted them. Thus Jonas A. Barish demonstrates how three influential readings of the work of Shakespeare and his contemporaries result directly from their authors' own preconceptions, implying both the troublesome richness of a drama that can lend itself to such various interpretation and the hope that our modes of reconstruction can ultimately lead us back to an understanding of the plays according to the paradigms that governed their original audiences. Max Bluestone's study of *Doctor Faustus* concentrates on the dominant trends in criticism of Marlowe's play in order to make clear the central matters of the play as a theatrical experience that the traditional modes of criticism have almost universally ignored. Daniel Seltzer focuses on the way in which a play necessarily calls into legitimate creative life the imagination of the player, the director, the audience, and therefore necessarily demands some kind of distortion in performance. Through a series of entries in a theatergoer's notebook, Robert Hapgood's essay suggests that Shakespeare (who probably anticipated all our paradigms) is aware enough of the subjective role of the spectator in the making of the play to have virtually included him in the plays. In what will surely be a controversial reading of *Hamlet*, Stephen Booth reopens

questions that one might have imagined settled, simply by attend-
ing closely to what he argues must be our experience as the play
creates an opening set of expectations and then bit by bit adds to,
plays on, fulfills or disappoints, and modifies those expectations.
And John Russell Brown provides a theoretical basis for such
analysis by demanding of criticism a new "theatrical understanding" which opens questions rather than closes them; he argues
that the inner life of a play, irreducible to "meaning," is accessible only to the theatrical audience, the critic who can actually
mount a production, or a theater of the mind.

If one cannot be sure of the direction in which the criticism
adumbrated by the essays gathered here is likely to move, one
must recognize that these six essays have managed themselves to
say new things about old plays. More important, it is extraordinary that for all their obvious differences of temperament and
technique the writers, assigned a general topic of "Reinterpretations of Elizabethan Drama," should have found such a common
voice for the new things they have to say. Their shared assumptions speak for what is likely to be a period of rediscovery and
of new understanding of the value of what we have always cared
for. And it is evidence, if we needed it, of the astonishing vitality
of Shakespeare and his contemporaries that their work should so
naturally become a focus for a fresh approach to the problem of
literary interpretation.

NORMAN RABKIN

University of California, Berkeley
March, 1969

Contents

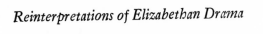

Reinterpretations of Elizabethan Drama

Jonas A. Barish

THE NEW THEATER AND THE OLD:

REVERSIONS AND REJUVENATIONS

MY TITLE ALLUDES TO William Archer's manifesto of realism, *The Old Drama and the New* (1923), which I take to represent, with as much lucidity and cogency as possible, one extreme position toward the Elizabethan drama. Its polar opposite I would represent by another manifesto, Antonin Artaud's *The Theater and Its Double*, published fifteen years later, in 1938. Artaud had probably not read a word of Archer, had very likely never heard of him. Moreover, he does not set out expressly to champion the old drama as Archer sets about to demolish it. At the same time his own notions of the theater derive to some extent from his study of the Elizabethans, and he dreams of reviving them as part of his projected reform of the stage. Furthermore, his book challenges Archer's theses so frontally, on so many levels and even in so many particulars, that the two seem to emerge as embodiments of two antithetic views of drama stemming in turn from two primordially divergent visions of life. As a third cardinal point I would take Bertolt

Brecht, a pupil of the Elizabethans in a different way from Artaud; Brecht's interests cut across the rather simple dichotomy set up by the other two and produce a more complicated map of the same terrain. My purpose is simply to explore this configuration of attitudes through a glance at these representative figures. My subtitle alludes to some stage adaptations, which I should like to look at to help discover the spirit in which recent authors have turned back to the Elizabethans, and the kinds of fresh energies they have tried to release from them.

As for the Elizabethan drama itself, although Archer assails it and Artaud espouses it, it does not occupy quite so simple a position as those simple facts might lead one to expect. We may take it as axiomatic that any generation will revaluate the literature of the past in the light of its own preoccupations; it will listen for the vibrations that chime with its own. Our own generation, and its immediate predecessors, have been multiple and eclectic in their preoccupations. And what they have heard in the Elizabethan drama has been its eclecticism and multifariousness. Looked at through twentieth-century sensibilities, the Elizabethan drama preserves a certain chameleon quality. It appears to be now one thing, now another—very like a camel, a weasel, or a whale, depending on one's angle of squint. It merges elements of the theater of realism with that of unrealism in quixotic and unpredictable combinations; it strives for verisimilitude in the very moment in which it is practicing the most extreme conventionality.

Its grand antagonist, Archer, we should note, in intellectual temper belongs to the late nineteenth century. Archer is an impenitent rationalist, furious with Christianity for foisting onto the world for so long its ridiculous myths—its "folklore"—and then for persisting in them after they have been so definitively discredited by the successive discoveries of astronomy, geology, anthropology, and textual criticism. "The true religion," he believes, "is to avail ourselves of our almost unlimited power of shaping human conditions in accordance with the enlightened human will."[1] True drama, evidently, would further the same grand design. Its past already illustrates the power of the enlightened will in human affairs, embodying as it does a process of purification in which, over the centuries, it has purged itself of its irrational elements—its mythic and lyric impurities, everything that links it to its chthonic origins—so that it might arrive at the distilled perfections of Pinero, Jones, Galsworthy, and Granville-Barker. Not the least token of the superiority of these last-named dramatists is their own faith in social betterment. In their plays they have inscribed their commitment to progress, and helped to effectuate a modicum of it.

Archer measures the drama, as he measures religion and philosophy, by the canons of logic. True drama, as he conceives it, aspires toward imitation, faithful and consistent imitation, of the visible and audible surfaces of life.[2] The function of the stage is to look as much as possible like the "real" house it pretends to be; the aim of the actor is to behave as nearly as possible like his real

---

[1] J. M. Robertson, ed., *William Archer as Rationalist* (London, 1925), pp. 81, 47, 85.

[2] *The Old Drama and the New* (New York, 1923), pp. 16, 13, 135, 18. Quotations used by permission of Dodd, Mead & Company.

counterpart on the other side of the footlights; and the goal of dramatic dialogue is to be indistinguishable from the speech of the marketplace. What Archer recoils from in the Elizabethan drama is not merely its illogicality and its peremptory ways with narrative but the very quality of its insight—its lyrical, passional side, the element of "wilful, sometimes hysterical exaggeration" with which the dramatists invested their plots, the "cothurnate speech"[3] of the characters, those speeches so exasperatingly like songs, and so little like believable parlor conversation. "The task which reason prescribes to the dramatic artist is to exhibit character by the same means by which it manifests itself in real life"[4] —not only without recourse to asides and soliloquies and the rest of the apparatus of make-believe in which the Elizabethan drama abounded, but also without eloquence: dramatic characters ought to be no more articulate than ordinary people. Juliet, left alone by Romeo after their wedding night, is forbidden by the conventions of Elizabethan dramaturgy to do what any normal girl would do in the circumstances—to throw herself on the bed in tears. She has no choice but to adopt another convention and "fall back upon words."[5] So Shakespeare proceeds to weave pretty poetic arabesques to replace the real thing. For authentic expressiveness we are referred to Pinero's Letty, who receives the news that the man she hopes to marry is married already with the strangled phrase, "You might have mentioned it before. You might have mentioned it." Here, declares Archer exultantly, "we have no oratory, no lyric cry, but pure double-distilled drama. We feel the anguish, the precipitous fall from hope to despair,

[3] *Ibid.*, pp. 5, 8.   [4] *Ibid.*, p. 41.   [5] *Ibid.*, p. 125.

that lie behind the simple phrases: 'You might have mentioned it before. You might have mentioned it.' "[6] The emotion thus lodges somewhere behind the spoken phrases, not in them. It is wholly a function of context; nothing is articulated or realized, except perhaps by the virtuosity of the actress. Again, in Stanley Houghton's *Hindle Wakes*, when Fanny discovers that her parents know she has lied to them concerning her weekend escapade, and discovers in the same moment that the friend she has been using as an alibi has drowned over the week-end—when she learns all this, says Archer, we can "imagine the torrent of emotion which sweeps over Fanny's mind."[7] It is the audience, then, or the reader, who is to do the imagining, not the playwright. Very much like the Edwardian novelists arraigned by Virginia Woolf, Pinero is trying to make us imagine for him. He and the other playwrights writing for the box set, with its walls and carpets and solid furniture, its butlers and clinking dinner plates, are "trying to hypnotise us into the belief that, because [they have] made a house, there must be a person living there."[8]

As Archer is seduced by the sham psychology of Pinero and the realists, because their characters inhabit a stage cluttered with familiar household objects and never digress into poetry, so he finds Elizabethan characters implausible because they act abruptly, in frequent defiance of common sense, and with the bizarre intensity of creatures of parable. Thus he judges *Volpone* to be essentially false because Jonson has so exaggerated the fol-

[6] *Ibid.*, p. 122.   [7] *Ibid.*, p. 124.
[8] Virginia Woolf, *Mr. Bennett and Mrs. Brown* (London, 1924), p. 16.

lies of his characters. Avarice, in Archer's home-grown psychology, coexists with parsimony but never with generosity; the legacy-hunters would never lavish so many gifts on their proposed victim; gulls are not so preternaturally gullible; people don't do those things. Similarly, the psychic workings of the Aragonian brothers, in *The Duchess of Malfi*, remain incomprehensible because they have "no rational motive" for objecting to their sister's remarriage, and Calantha's behavior, in the dance climax of *The Broken Heart*, is "a piece of funereal affectation."[9] No one would behave as Calantha does, nor would we admire her if she did, for her callousness at this juncture outrages decency. What Archer requires, to slake his raging thirst for logic, is that a rational motive be prescribed, or be capable of being unequivocally inferred, for every dramatic event. And that that motive be one that would instantly persuade an Englishman of the early twentieth century, with a good job and a steady income, of its validity. Everything surprising, contradictory, bewildering in human nature, whatever declines to submit to ledger and roster, is ruled out of court as unnatural.

Archer does find guarded words of approval for a handful of Elizabethan plays, among them *The Changeling*, because of its intrinsically sound dramatic situation, and Massinger's comedy *The Great Duke of Florence*, which has the signal merit of being something that "might have been written by a gentleman."[10] But he finds both sadly wanting in logic, and undertakes to correct their shortcomings by rewriting them under the new titles of *Beatriz-Juana* and *Lidia*. The aim is pedagogical—to give the

[9] *The Old Drama and the New*, pp. 84, 53, 65.
[10] *Ibid.*, p. 108.

Elizabethan playwrights a belated lesson in dramaturgy, as it were, to rescue the valuable elements in their plays from the "technical and spiritual crudities of a semi-barbarous age" by reconceiving the action "in the light of . . . the more civilized theatrical methods of today." "The theoretical point I set out to prove was that dramatic creation, as we nowadays understand it, demands a form of intellectual effort totally different from that of the Elizabethans, and far more complex. . . . they were specifically poets rather than dramatists; whereas I am, or try to be, specifically a dramatist, and not a poet."[11]

The theoretical point which Archer in fact succeeded in proving was that the dramatist could not do without a touch of the poet. In both cases he tidies the narrative; he prunes irrelevancies and expunges improbabilities. Motivation is rationalized throughout. There remain no disconcerting plunges into paradox, such as Beatrice-Joanna's choosing for her accomplice in murder the one man she most completely loathes and has provided with signal grounds for resentment. The psychological acuteness of Middleton's conception is lost on Archer because it involves a logical inconsistency. One wonders what he made of Beatrice-Joanna's words of self-discovery in the final moments, "My loathing/ Was prophet to the rest." At all events he replaces the ugly ruffianly De Flores with a trusty family retainer who years ago has been treated contemptuously by Beatriz-Juana, and so harbors hidden cause for anger against her, but who currently embodies just the right amalgam of familiarity and servility to make him a plausible instrument. Archer makes him more plausible still by providing him with his own motive for the murder:

11 *Three Plays* (New York, 1927), pp. 93–95.

he is the target of insults from Beatriz-Juana's official suitor, a braggart for whom Beatriz-Juana herself shows open scorn. The whole murky process by which Middleton's heroine comes to an awareness of herself, the horrifying mingle of sleepwalking and animal cunning, is replaced by an arithmetic of motive and countermotive. From this basis we proceed to an intricate super-structure of props and clues—jeweled daggers and empty wells and letters of assignation. The plot turns into a detective story seen from the inside, with the bits of evidence being manufac-tured and manipulated before our eyes by the criminals. The result is a perfectly workmanlike dramatic fable, without a breath of life stirring anywhere in it. By his relentless explaining and accounting Archer has emptied the story of the fierce insight it had in Middleton, and even of the suspense with which, in Mid-dleton, we watched events whose outcome we could foresee. Archer proves not how demanding the prescripts of rationalism can be, but how deadly. Nor can we suppose it coincidence that the process that so expertly constructs false limbs should end by producing a robot.

One may make essentially the same point about the conver-sion of *The Great Duke of Florence* into *Lidia:* Archer has turned Massinger's delicate but vigorous little play of awakening passion into a crepe-paper sugarplum. The deletion of the up-surge of erotic feeling from the ducal ambassador, so as to reduce him to a harmless witty uncle, removes all real danger from the dramatic situation. The substitution for the gravely aristocratic Princess of the vulgar Marchesa, like an overbearing English ma-tron stalking a suitable match for a hoydenish daughter, imports a host of trivializing complications into the story. The Marchesa's doings quickly come to have as much predictability as those of a figure from musical comedy. In his effort to do away with the stereotypes of an earlier age, Archer has simply substituted the more banal clichés of his own.

Shaw's rewriting of Act v of *Cymbeline* affords a more complicated but roughly analogous case. With his sharper instinct for theater, Shaw labored under no such hampering assumptions as Archer concerning the inherent desirability of logic; *Cymbeline Refinished* preserves in any case the character of a *jeu d'esprit*. Yet it betrays a surprising tinge of Archerian literalism. Shaw objects, as he informs us in his Preface, to the "ludicrous" stage battle (by which he can only mean its inadequacy as realism), the foolishness of the romance device of the mole on his neck to identify Guiderius, and the collapse of believability in the dramatis personae toward the end. "With one exception," he complains, "the characters have vanished and left nothing but dolls being moved about like the glass balls in the game of solitaire until they are all got rid of but one."[12] Shaw galvanizes the glass dolls by making them into Shavian puppets. Imogen becomes a manifestation of the life force, a standard-bearer for wronged femininity, wrangling with Posthumus over his unjust suspicions; Iachimo becomes a chocolate soldier, prompt with jests on such matters as his uncomfortable night of confinement in the trunk. The death of the queen is omitted, as smacking too much of fairy tale, thus depriving us of the one vivid reminder of evil in the scene. Similarly—because no audience could credit it for an instant—the identification of Guiderius by the mole on his neck is

---

[12] *Geneva, Cymbeline Refinished, & Good King Charles* (London, 1946), p. 135.

omitted, thus depriving us of the most striking instance of the beneficent workings of chance. The result, as with Archer's Middleton, is that the operation that removes the tumor kills the patient. The very thing that the rational mind sees as an excrescence, the magical strain in the story, proves to contain its lifeblood. Shakespeare's solemn ritual of conclusion, with its ceremonious rhythm and its moments of wonder, has been converted into an outburst of triviality that disfigures the entire play.

But one did not need to be skeptical of the Elizabethans to deform their plays in the guise of readying them for production. Some of the most notorious butchery was perpetrated by William Poel, who instructed his whole generation in the need of the platform stage for Elizabethan revivals. Even Shaw and Archer stood aghast at Poel's highhanded way with his texts, and one can understand why when one looks at such things as his reworking of *Arden of Feversham* under the title of *Lilies That Fester*. The play is renamed because, according to Poel, "it has been almost entirely reconstructed to allow of its being acted on the modern stage," the excuse for the reconstruction in turn being the alleged fact that "by our early English playwrights the art of dramatic construction was still but little understood. A unity or design is wanting, as well as continuity of action leading directly to a climax."[13] To achieve this wanting unity, Poel seizes the language of the play as if it were movie film and goes to work with scissors. Speeches are transferred from one place to another, reassigned, spliced together; episodes are dropped, relocated, shortened, hooked into and out of each other with a kind

[13] *Lilies That Fester and Love's Constancy* (New York, 1906), Introduction, pp. iii, v.

of lunatic abandon that leaves one giddy. One may grant that the design of *Arden of Feversham* lacks subtlety, that it follows the vicissitudes of its chronicle source with occasionally comic fidelity. At the same time it is from the cumulative technique and the homiletic impulse of the chronicle that the play derives most of its considerable power. Poel's snug little one-acter, by contrast, set in the manor parlor and starting in the middle of things, conducts us for no apparent reason through a certain sequence of events, and then, still for no discernible reason, stops. Like Archer's rewritings of Middleton and Massinger it does not really seem to be *about* anything. The reshuffling of the material into its arbitrary new form, however, underscores the fact that the anonymous Elizabethan playwright did write with a purpose —if a confused one—attempting to dramatize a crime both of passion and of retribution, with a second phase of retribution following hard upon the consummation of the crime, and at some points coextensive with it. The purpose has eluded the adapter, and Poel's clever carpentry produces an effect similar to that of some nineteenth-century restorations of Gothic cathedrals, where the reordering of them to achieve a spurious neatness has ended by producing a truly bewildering and incoherent object.

We discover, then, at this moment in the Elizabethan revival, a patronizing attitude toward Elizabethan dramaturgy, especially toward its more Gothic features, its irregularities and redundancies. The double plot is assumed to be a relic of barbarism; its aesthetic potentialities remain unrecognized. It goes without saying that Archer, in his version of *The Changeling*, eliminates Rowley's madmen. But Maeterlinck, in his celebrated translation of *'Tis Pity She's a Whore* in 1894, under the title *Annabella*, does the same: he omits both subplots, and considers himself to have done playgoers a favor. He has disengaged, he says, the "very simple and very human" tragedy of the lovers from its surrounding tissue, as one would remove a diamond from its matrix of ore; he has separated it as one might separate a noble flower from parasitic growths that have no roots in common with it.[14] One may share Maeterlinck's distaste for these particular subplots, with their murky intrigues and their otiose masques and poisonings, and still feel that he has made the very simple tragedy somewhat too simple with this procedure. By removing it from its setting in an ignoble society he has removed the network of stresses within which the lovers found themselves trapped. The last fifty lines are now gone in which, in Ford, the frigid Cardinal, presiding over the carnage of the banquet, seizes, for the Church's use, the treasure left by the deceased persons, and metes out unequal justice to the survivors. The spectacle of order being restored by an official without a shred of moral authority revives our sympathies for the incestuous lovers at the ultimate moment, and envelops their career in heavy irony. It sheds on their perverse liaison some of the feverish glitter of a thing seen under phosphorescent light. Maeterlinck's exclusions tends to emphasize the fragility of the lovers rather than their heroism. By cutting their story adrift from its social moorings,

[14] *Annabella* (Paris, 1895), Preface, pp. xviii–xix. See also Marcel Schwob's lecture at the Théâtre de l'Oeuvre, on the occasion of the production, in which he praises the translator for relieving the play of a secondary plot "which only served to obscure the principal action," so that it now has taken on the aspect of a Greek tragedy, where nothing interferes with the forward propulsion of the story. *Mercure de France*, XII (1894), 332.

he makes it into something resembling his own poetic dramas of the same decade, one of those tales in which lost creatures, faint of outline, wander hopelessly through crepuscular forests and expire silently in far-off dim châteaux.

Jacques Copeau's decision to delete the subplot of *A Woman Killed with Kindness* for performance at the Vieux-Colombier in 1913 is more surprising still. Perhaps his attention had been caught by Maeterlinck's admiring words on the play, in the preface to *Annabella*: "this masterpiece," Maeterlinck calls it, "this first family tragedy, and more painful than any other because it is so simply quotidian."[15] Copeau's alterations certainly work to enhance the quotidian aspect of the play. Doubtless he abandoned the second plot, involving the tribulations of Sir Charles Mountford, in conformance with the taste of the time, which found Elizabethan plays overloaded. But in so doing, he also dropped most of the improbabilities, the melodramatic self-sacrifice of Susan Mountford and the miraculous conversion of Sir Francis Acton, so that the main story moves more into the domain of the bourgeois *drame à thèse*, a whole system of cross-lights and ironic reflections between the two plots being blacked out, as it were, by the simple throwing of a switch. Poel, refashioning *Arden of Feversham*, had spoken of his hope of "bringing back into popular favour this lurid Kentish tragedy . . . one of the comparatively few plays of the sixteenth century in which the plot and action are founded upon English life and manners."[16] Archer's terms of approbation for the same plays are even more revealing:

15 *Annabella*, Preface, p. x.
16 *Lilies That Fester*, Introduction, p. vii.

> Elizabethan tragedy now and then showed a disposition to put off the cothurnus and apply itself to the sober imitation of life. Such a play as *Arden of Feversham* anticipated by a century and a half some . . . of the theories of Diderot, and offered a specimen of the bourgeois drama. So, too, Heywood's *A Woman Killed with Kindness* anticipated in its essence, though not in its form, some of the problem plays of modern times.[17]

What Copeau is doing, in effect, is making Heywood's play resemble more closely, in its form as well as in its essence, the problem plays of modern times, by taming the Elizabethan impetuosities of its dramaturgy. Even this pioneer in the retheatricalization of the theater, even such a proponent of symbolism as Maeterlinck, when they come to translate their enthusiasm for the Elizabethans into concrete stage practice, betray a lingering prejudice in favor of the logic of the quotidian that stamps them as contemporaries of Archer.

From our own point of vantage in time, Archer's summons to reason sounds like the rallying of a rearguard action in behalf of a lost cause. Nearly half a century had gone by since Zola had sounded the tocsin for naturalism in the theater, and in the intervening years the drama of the quotidian had flourished and started to decline. Most of the major theatrical talents had veered away from stage realism, and from the faith it implied in the superior reality of the visible and audible surfaces of daily life. Even Stanislavsky had retreated from an external to an interior realism. In Antonin Artaud, therefore, in the 1930s, we have a belated prophet arising to deliver fulminations against a dying

[17] *The Old Drama and the New*, p. 18.

tradition. Like Archer, Artaud seems to exemplify his own tradition with a peculiar intensity and clarity. The two indeed form
a remarkable contrast; no contraries hold more antipathy than
this apostle of progress with this votary of primitivism. What
Archer champions, Artaud despises and denounces; what Archer
spurns, Artaud fervently embraces. It is a kind of primal antago-
nism between everything sane and balanced and reasonable, and
everything furious, impassioned, and demonic. Artaud's aversion
to realism fully matches Archer's adherence to it. He is as pro-
grammatically bent on reinstating myth and ritual in the theater
as Archer is determined to extirpate them. What Artaud would
root out would be psychologism: "Psychology," he declares,
"which works relentlessly to reduce the unknown to the known,
to the quotidian and the ordinary, is the cause of the theater's
abasement and its fearful loss of energy."[18] It would be hard to
find the case against psychological drama more tellingly put, or a
sharper suggestion as to why the fixation on motive produces
effects so empty and unreal. Reduced to the known, to the mun-
dane and the ordinary, human nature ceases to be recognizable.
What we require to apprehend it as human is precisely the mys-
teriousness that Archer would banish from it. Artaud reverses
Archer's perspective of the history of drama. Far from being a
triumphal progress in his eyes, it is a steady deterioration, for
which Shakespeare himself, with his genius for storytelling psychology, must be held responsible. What Artaud demands by
way of antidote is a theater of shock and ecstasy, addressed not
to the spectator's mind or judgment but to his nerves and affec-

[18] *The Theater and Its Double*, trans. Mary Caroline Richards
(New York, 1958), p. 77. Copyright © 1958 by Grove Press, Inc.

tive apparatus. Artaud would turn the spectator into a snake hypnotized by a snake charmer. All strange and terrible events would be welcome, but the trivialities of the quotidian would be despised. The premium would be on "danger," or "anarchy," on the "impossible."

In such a theater moderation has no place. It becomes a virtue to push gestures as far as they will go. The lyric strain that Archer wished to purge from dramatic dialogue is to be reinstalled in the place of honor. Incantation becomes the aim, with words freed from their denotative fetters and used as blocks of pure sound. To some degree Artaud suits his own use of words to this poetic conception of them, so that his book proceeds in pulsations and flashes, through image and aphorism, rather than according to argumentative logic. Renouncing the conceptual tyranny of language, Artaud would renounce the superstitious veneration in which the texts of plays had traditionally been held, and restore to the *mise-en-scène* its presumptive sovereignty as orchestrator of the expressive alphabets of sound and color and space into a single total theatrical vocabulary.

The live example that Artaud comes to set up against the decaying European drama is the dance theater of the East, especially that of Bali, which he saw when it visited Paris in 1932. Here he discovered a valid antithesis to the theater of the quotidian. The Balinese dancers did not actually wear masks, but they used their faces in a peculiarly masklike way, rolling their eyes, pouting their lips, and contorting their facial muscles so as to depersonalize their faces. Similarly they used their limbs not to simulate real gestures but in a vocabulary of ritual motion that "excluded all idea of pretence, or cheap imitations of reality."

Instead of external events they portrayed inner states, "ossified and transformed into gestures—diagrams."[19] The whole purport of their art was magical, symbolical, "absolute."

For analogous reasons Yeats had already sought to copy the Japanese Noh drama, finding in its masks a nobler form of feeling than that available to individual faces. Gordon Craig had called for an "*Über-Marionette*" to replace the egoistic individual actor. And Eugene O'Neill had proclaimed his allegiance to "the one true theatre, the age-old theatre, the theatre of the Greeks and the Elizabethans,"[20] and looked to masks for various exalting and purifying functions, including the revitalizing of the art of acting. Archer, predictably, disparages the same phenomena, berating Noh drama and Chinese theater for the vices he dislikes in the Elizabethans. "Everywhere," he complains, "we find exaggeration, intensification, lording it over upon simple imitation—one halfpennyworth of imitative bread to an intolerable deal of exaggerative stock."[21] A certain consistency thus obtains between attitudes toward the Elizabethans on the one hand and the oriental dancers on the other: both constitute, for their admirers, a source of expressive lyricism and high stylization that holds promise of renewal for the moribund psychological theater of the West.

Artaud does not discuss the corpus of Elizabethan drama as such, and much of it clearly does not interest him. But certain plays recur in his writings as touchstones by which the true pos-

[19] *Ibid.*, p. 53.
[20] Toby Cole, ed., *Playwrights on Playwriting* (New York, 1960), p. 70.
[21] *The Old Drama and the New*, p. 8.

sibilities of the theater may be gauged, and foremost among them the plays of the Jacobean tragedians whom Maeterlinck designated as "the black princes of horror," Tourneur, Webster, and Ford.[22] To illustrate the resemblance between the theater and the plague, Artaud chooses as demonstration piece *'Tis Pity She's a Whore*. Here he finds one character, Giovanni, "heroically criminal and audaciously, ostentatiously heroic," for whom no barriers exist, and another, Annabella, who embodies "the absolute condition of revolt," "an exemplary case of love without respite which makes us, the spectators, gasp with anguish at the idea that nothing will ever be able to stop it." He outlines the action as follows: "With them [Giovanni and Annabella] we proceed from excess to excess and vindication to vindication. Annabella is captured, convicted of adultery and incest, trampled upon, insulted, dragged by the hair, and we are astonished to discover that far from seeking a means of escape, she provokes her executioner still further and sings out in a kind of obstinate heroism."[23]

But is this an accurate account? When we turn back to the play, we discover that Annabella's revolt is far from absolute. It is subject indeed to wild fluctuations. Artaud maintains silence about her remorse, her penitential tears brought on by the Friar's upbraidings, the soliloquy in which she speaks in bitter terms of her sinful state and vows to forsake the path of lust for that of conscience. The scene with Soranzo, cited by Artaud as evidence of her defiance, is in fact the only one of its kind, and expresses mainly her contempt for her accuser, not her indifference to the accusation. Otherwise, and increasingly toward the end, Anna-

[22] *Annabella*, Preface, p. viii.
[23] *The Theater and Its Double*, pp. 28–29.

bella leaves defiance to Giovanni. And we feel it to be a potentially disintegrating element in their situation that they are so
unequal in resolve, that Giovanni's grim fixity must contend
with his sister's vacillations. The tension between them threatens
to undo them from within, as the world conspires to destroy
them from without. Artaud, in trying to reduce the plot to a
single unvarying motif, has lopped off one significant dimension
of it, and so falsified it.

On *The Revenger's Tragedy* Archer can scarcely contain
his execrations. This play, the product of a "sanguinary maniac,"
a creature with "a hideous mind, [who] dealt in hideous themes,
and revelled in hideous language"—can it be said to belong to
"civilized literature" at all?[24] "Civilized literature" is the formula
of approval that comes naturally to Archer. It embodies the criterion of civility by which he judges plays, and it views them as
a branch of letters. For Artaud the theater should neither be
civilized nor be literature. It should impinge on us physically. It
should uncover rather than dissemble our latent barbarism, treating us like psychoanalytic patients, making us reenact our deep
terrors and drives so as to rid ourselves of the compulsion to act
them in our daily lives. To effect this catharsis it must be compounded precisely of the images of horror to be found in the
Jacobean tragic dramatists. Artaud designates *The Revenger's
Tragedy, The White Devil, The Duchess of Malfi,* and (doubtless more for its violence than its domesticity) *Arden of Feversham* as plays for revival first at the Théâtre Jarry, and then,
upon the collapse of that venture, at the even more abortive
Théâtre de la Cruauté. They are to be interpreted, however, not

24 *The Old Drama and the New,* pp. 73, 70, 74.

as with Maeterlinck and Copeau through scrupulous translation, but through radical reformulation, stripped down to their constituents and then freely recomposed to form a total spectacle.

As for the physical conditions of Artaud's theater, they are to reverse those of the theater of realism. For Archer the aim of drama was to provide men with credible imitations of their own lives and so assist them in their spiritual progress. For this purpose he found the picture stage a perfect instrument. The proscenium arch, by imposing an absolute separation between stage and spectators, encouraged the former to become an exact mirror image of the latter, and the realistic set, so closely duplicating the thing it claimed to represent, forbade the irresponsible author to resort to asides, soliloquies, and other unnatural shortcuts. Artaud would abolish the duality of stage and auditorium and replace them by a single continuous site, without boundary or partition. The spectator, a detached observer no longer, would be engulfed by the spectacle, bombarded by colors, lights, and sounds. About him would swirl huge masks, giant mannekins, hieroglyphics, objects "of strange proportions," and creatures in "ritual costumes."[25] All this so as to subvert his judgment and his normal sense of himself, send seismic shock waves coursing through him, to teach him his helplessness in face of the powers that rule human destiny.

Artaud never succeeded in staging an Elizabethan play. He did, however, produce a pseudo-Elizabethan play, for the first and (as it proved) only production of his second directorial enterprise, the so-called Theater of Cruelty. The play, *The Cenci*, Artaud directed with himself in the main role, in a version based

[25] *The Theater and Its Double*, p. 97.

on Shelley and freely reworked with the aid of the original documents as transcribed and glossed by Stendhal. I think we may take his dealings with it as evidence of what he would have done with a play by Ford or Webster or Tourneur. By his own admission this first essay at a new theater involved many compromises; it did not get beyond a preliminary sketch of what he hoped to work out more radically in the future. But some tentative observations may be hazarded, and first on the term "cruelty." Artaud uses this word poetically, disdaining to be tied to the customary meanings. He shows frequent exasperation with those who think that by cruelty he means physical violence, when in fact he means a condition of the spirit. "From the point of view of the mind," he declares, "cruelty signifies rigor, implacable intention and decision, irreversible and absolute determination."[26] This implacable intention, as we have noticed, is what he finds, more indeed than the text warrants, in 'Tis Pity She's a Whore. It is also what he unearths from and expatiates on in the career of Count Cenci. But both times the cruelty that starts as a spiritual state descends ultimately to the physical sphere, where it does result in bodily mutilation. For Artaud, correctly as I think, the tearing out of Annabella's heart and the brandishing of it at sword's point before the banquet guests marks the last stage in the progress of Giovanni's will, and the final proof of its relentlessness.

We may expect, then, that he will deal with the Cenci story more in Ford's manner than in Shelley's, and this proves to be the case. Shelley wishes, so he says, to unveil the dark and secret caverns of the human heart, but he prefers to muffle the cruelties in the story so as to shield the reader from the wrong kind of

[26] *Ibid.*, p. 101.

excitement. "The person who would treat such a subject," he explains, "must increase the ideal, and diminish the actual horror of the events," so that the pleasure felt in the poetry may mitigate the discomfort felt at the sight of so much evil.[27] Artaud proceeds otherwise. In the historical account, Count Cenci was killed by having two nails driven into his head as he slept—one through his eye and one through his throat. Shelley softens this grisly detail by having the Count strangled. Artaud restores the historical circumstance, but departs from history by providing two sinister mutes as the cutthroats rather than the loquacious assassins of Shelley. Instead of keeping the whole sequence offstage, moreover, he brings Count Cenci back before our eyes, streaming blood, staggering, and clutching at his eye where the nail has been hammered in; as this is happening, "terrible fanfares" fill the air at a deafening volume. In Shelley, again, the conclusion dissolves into a wilderness of rhetoric, with plea, counterplea, defiance, and despair succeeding one another. Artaud substitutes a prison scene in which Beatrice is tortured onstage, fettered and manacled and hanging by her hair from a wheel on the ceiling, which drags her about with it as it rotates. We may infer, then, that while cries, bloodshed, and torment may not, for Artaud, constitute the essence of cruelty, they form a nearly inevitable accompaniment to it; they supply the guarantee of the remorselessness of spirit which defines it, both in the tormentors and in the tormented.

Structurally, *Les Cenci* is of an extreme, even a skeletal spareness, far more Senecan than Elizabethan. The dense contin-

[27] *Selected Poetry and Prose*, ed. Carlos Baker (New York, 1951), p. 448.

uum of sounds and lighting effects has crowded out plot as well as text, reducing both to a kind of simple conceptual armature. We may recall that Artaud revered Seneca as the supreme exponent of written tragedy, and it is plainly the Senecan side of the Elizabethan drama that attracts him, its willingness to push pain and horror to their uttermost. He admires it, then, on a narrow basis, not for its language or its plotting or its texture, or for any of its own ways of conveying its vision—except perhaps the use of stage torture—but for the white-hot center of that vision, the spectacle of doomed creatures, in the Jacobean tragedies, rushing furiously toward their own damnation.

The playwright who has shown himself responsive to the structural properties of the Elizabethan drama, and eager to emulate them, has been Brecht, whom we may take as a spokesman of a different sort from Artaud. We might think of him as forming the third point in an equilateral triangle, with Archer and Artaud the other two. Artaud shares with Archer a belief in something fundamental called human nature, though one locates it in reason and the other in instinctual drives and primordial imaginings. Both would subscribe to T. S. Eliot's dictum that the best Elizabethan plays provide us with a profound vision of abiding human dilemmas.[28] Brecht, resolutely Marxist on this as on other points, does not believe in a fixed human nature or abiding dilemmas, but only in historical problems and processes, in particular men acting for specific purposes at precise moments in time. The Elizabethan playwrights, to the extent that they deal with the archaic passions of kings and other feudal leaders, do not interest him, nor should they, in his view, interest us. Brecht would have the

[28] *Selected Essays 1917–32* (New York, 1932), pp. 142, 144.

theater explore such men as historical beings, show them as the products of the social forces that shape them, and as the agents or opponents of change. For this un-Elizabethan purpose he finds the Elizabethan chronicle play a congenial model; it liberates the playwright from the despotism of unified structure and leaves him free to present a situation from many aspects, to tighten and relax tension, to vary style and tempo. Brecht would accept Archer's charge that Elizabethan dramaturgy is often undramatic, but he would give "undramatic" an honorific twist by rechristening it "epic." "With an epic work, as opposed to a dramatic," he points out, "one can as it were take a pair of scissors and cut it into individual pieces, which remain fully capable of life."[29] Like Wölfflin's category of "Renaissance" as opposed to "baroque," the chronicle form thrives on independence of parts. When Brecht remakes Marlowe's *Edward II*, far from trying to soften the chronicle aspect he heightens it by using historical captions at the beginning of each scene, to remind the spectators that they are witnessing remote events, with which they need not too ardently identify.

At the root of Brecht's preference for chronicle form lies

[29] *Brecht on Theatre*, trans. John Willett (London, 1964), p. 70. Probably a further exception to the prevailing misunderstanding of Elizabethan dramaturgy would be found in Meyerhold, one of Brecht's mentors, who saw *Hamlet* as a sublimer instance of the kind of structure typified in *Cambises*. Meyerhold's constructivism, according to one of his commentators, may itself be traced back to earlier forms of staging, especially the Elizabethan, and his most famous constructivist spectacle, the giant machine of *Le cocu magnifique*, merely adapts the forestage, rear stage, and balcony of the Elizabethan playhouse. Meyerhold *et al.*, *Le théâtre théâtral*, trans. Nina Gourfinkel (Paris, 1963), pp. 124–25, 165.

his well-known distaste for the playwright as spellbinder. Archer would have had dramatists cultivate realistic illusion until the events onstage became indistinguishable from those off, and the spectator responded accordingly, with total empathy. Artaud sought to induce trance, delirium, and hallucination, as a way of discharging the spectator of his toxic excesses. Brecht's antithetic ideal of judicious detachment is symbolized by the man who smokes while watching a play. Lighting his cigar, such a man reflects dispassionately on what he is witnessing, and his coolness works to dissipate amorphous surges of feeling. If he reacts, he does so with "social" sentiments, with hatred for injustice, perhaps, or indignation at tyranny, but not with the element of emotional projection that ordinarily accompanies theatrical experience, and certainly without the narcotic states desiderated by Artaud. He remains alertly critical of what he sees. He does not, like the entranced spectator, feel a conviction of the inevitability of the action, that it had to happen thus. Rather, he sees that things might have turned out otherwise. The hero, confronted with this or that choice, might have done this thing rather than that other.

The multiple role of the Elizabethan drama in the imaginations of our contemporaries is well illustrated by the fact that where Artaud saw in it a key to the unleashing of our subterranean demons, Brecht sees in it series of devices of disintoxication.

Nothing [he says] gives us a better idea of the sober, healthy, profane state of the Elizabethan theatre than a look at Shakespeare's contracts with his companies, which guaranteed him a seventh part of the shares and a fourteenth part

of the income of two theatres; at the cuts he made in his
own plays, amounting to between a quarter and a third of all
the verses; at his instructions to his actors (in *Hamlet*) to
act in a restrained and natural manner. Add to that the fact
that they acted (and also rehearsed, of course) by daylight
in the open air, mostly without any attempt to indicate the
place of the action and in the closest proximity to the audience, who sat on all sides, including on the stage, with a
crowd standing or strolling around, and you'll begin to get
an idea how earthly, profane and lacking in magic it all
was.[30]

The shareholding arrangements, then, backed up by the supposed
circumstances of production, build a certain dry practicality into
the whole venture, which counteracts the theater's insidious tendency to cast a spell. Elizabethan stage conventions serve the
same end. When the ghosts appear to Richmond and Richard in
the last act of *Richard III*, both leaders being on the stage in their
respective tents simultaneously, we have a capital instance of the
alienation effect. The episode works diagrammatically, with no
concern for mimetic realism. The devices that for Archer be-
longed among the deadly sins of the old drama have thus become
for Brecht its cardinal virtues, since they conspire to preserve
our disbelief instead of encouraging us to suspend it. What
Brecht does not allow for is that Elizabethan audiences, and playwrights, were dissatisfied with this state of affairs. They chafed
at the limits placed on theatrical illusion by daylight, primitive
scenery, and inattentive crowds, and they welcomed indoor

[30] *The Messingkauf Dialogues*, trans. John Willett (London,
1965), pp. 58–59. Quoted by permission of Methuen & Co. Ltd.

theater such as that at the Blackfriars precisely because it made possible some of the effects of glamorous make-believe that Brecht admires them for not caring about.

Brecht's apparent confusion on this point is the more surprising in that elsewhere he speaks eloquently of the mingled texture of Elizabethan drama, and harshly of the way its rich legacy has been thinned and narrowed:

> Take the element of conflict in Elizabethan plays, complex, shifting, largely impersonal, never soluble, and then see what has been made of it today, whether in contemporary plays or in contemporary renderings of the Elizabethans. Compare the part played by empathy then and now. What a contradictory, complicated and intermittent operation it was in Shakespeare's theatre![31]

What Brecht has in mind here, evidently, is the simple polarities of sympathy and antipathy in which the later drama came to deal, and which directors came to impose on Shakespearean productions. It is hard to imagine him reacting other than with impatience to Artaud's simplifications of Ford, which seem designed to iron out the "contradictory, complicated and intermittent" responses called for by the play itself, in favor of an unambiguous alignment of sympathies. For his own part, Brecht would prefer not to enlist sympathies at all, but to foster judgment. When he reconstructs an Elizabethan play, as he did on two occasions, he seeks to minimize the emotional stresses between character and spectator. Edward II becomes a figure more deserving of our respect than his prototype in Marlowe, but at the same

---

[31] *Brecht on Theatre,* p. 161.

time less able to make us share his sufferings. Brecht deletes his self-pitying eloquence and his outbursts of affection for his friends. Becoming more abrasive in speech, but also less given to neurotic indecision, he sets up fewer emotional vibrations in us. The usurper, Mortimer, analogously, becomes more devious, more expressly Machiavellian, but less antipathetic because less boastful and hubristic, more scholarly and more concerned for the welfare of the kingdom. Again, Baldock's Judaslike betrayal of his master, Brecht's own invention, is viewed largely in economic terms: Baldock has an old mother to care for, who must eat. We are not invited to wax indignant over his treachery, or to see it as a symptom of temperamental disloyalty, but to recognize it as a human response, if a distasteful one, to the pressure of circumstances. Brecht deters us at all points from throwing ourselves feelingly into the struggle, either with the barons when they smart under Edward's petulance, or on Edward's side when he falls victim to Mortimer's cruelty. Our attention swings away from the clash of personalities to a clash between styles of statecraft—old-fashioned absolutism against ministerial efficiency.

As with *Edward II*, near the beginning of Brecht's career, so with *Coriolanus*, on which he worked for four years before his death. Here was a play that seemed virtually ready-made for his purposes—notorious, indeed, among Shakespearean tragedies for its failure, or its refusal, to generate tragic empathy. But Brecht carries the process much further. Most of the emotional charge built up by Shakespeare in the confrontation between hero and tribunes is carefully defused. Coriolanus is made even more unyielding and laconic than before, and all the great crises in which he struggles with his feelings are dismantled of their tension.

While soliciting the votes of the people in the forum, instead of delivering a soliloquy he sings a sardonic ballad to the accompaniment of a bagpipe, "The Song of the Grateful She-Wolf." Instead, that is, of conscripting us into his cause by laying bare his feelings, he comments cynically on his own performance, forbidding us access to his feelings. In the scene in the Volscian camp he does not experience anything like the emotional upheaval of his Shakespearean original; his dilemma is never allowed to seem intolerable. He does not, at the climax, seize his mother's hand and hold it with mute intensity, nor does he confess immediately thereafter to Aufidius that the confrontation has wrung tears from him. Aufidius, in turn, no longer pays public tribute to his dead enemy after having him killed in the marketplace in Corioli. All the means utilized by Shakespeare to compel our admiration of Coriolanus and endow him with grandeur are sabotaged by Brecht. Coriolanus, in consequence, ceases to seem heroic, ceases to awe us, and becomes merely a somewhat alarming "specimen." Our good sense requires us to concur in the proposition that he could, had he wished, have acted otherwise, and that without him the city does become, as the tribunes assert, a more comradely place, worth saving for perhaps the first time in its history.

As for the tribunes, far from being the repellent Machiavels of Shakespeare, they emerge as the natural leaders of a populace much less hysterical than Shakespeare's. Instead of fomenting disruption to further their own selfish ends, they seek to clarify the issues dividing their faction from the patriciate, and to unify the plebians into an effective fighting force. It is they who assume the defense of the city when Coriolanus marches on it, while most of the aristocrats prepare to sit with folded hands waiting for the slaughter. The play now ends with an apocryphal scene in which they take over in businesslike fashion the conduct of affairs in the Senate, refusing to grant honors to the memory of Coriolanus or to confer the usual mourning privileges on his survivors. We no longer concern ourselves with the feudal spectacle of a great man brought low; we no longer involve ourselves intimately in the upsurge of his individuality and painfully cosuffer his fall. Rather, we ponder the difficult transition to a more valid form of government. We assess the penalties to the commonwealth of the activity of characters like Coriolanus. We learn, more from the people than from Menenius Agrippa, how a healthy society might function.

In both plays Brecht thus employs certain formal features of Elizabethan dramaturgy, but sets his own stamp on them. He repeats the working methods of the original playwrights, going back to the chronicles—Holinshed probably, Plutarch and Livy certainly—in order to restudy the characters, and ends with something profoundly different. By the time he has finished with his own version of the lives of Edward II and Coriolanus, we are less mindful of what drew him to these plays in the first place—their relatively dry treatment of their protagonists—than struck by how freely, and indeed almost automatically, even in these instances, the Elizabethan authors summoned up a passionate identification between audience and hero.

For varying purposes, then, the Elizabethan drama has been found sustaining and renewing in our own time. Successive generations have seen the old plays within the fields of force created by their own biases—first as an imperfect essay at realism, then as a triumph of antirealism, and finally as an artful mixture of both. They have attempted, similarly, first to domesticate the structure of the old plays to that of the well-made play, then to ignore that structure so as to concentrate on inner meaning, and finally to reproduce the structure so as to recover the original mode of apprehension. I would conclude, inconclusively, on a perhaps Archerian note of optimism by suggesting that this constitutes progress, that thanks to the polemics and experiments of our own stage we are drawing closer than at any time since the seventeenth century to an accurate perception of the theater of the Elizabethans.

Max Bluestone

Libido Speculandi: DOCTRINE AND DRAMATURGY
IN CONTEMPORARY INTERPRETATIONS
OF MARLOWE's *Doctor Faustus*

"WHAT MEANS THIS SHOW?" Faustus asks, when he is presented with the spectacle of the dancing devils. "Nothing," Mephostophilis assures him, "but to delight thy mind/ And let thee see what magic can perform."[1] The unsatiable speculator, as Marlowe's source calls him, Faustus here characteristically lusts after speculations, but he hears that spectacle suffices unto itself. Contemporary critical interpretation similarly speculates upon the meaning of Marlowe's tragical history of Faustus' life and death by asking Faustus' other question as well, "What doctrine call you this?" (i.47). So various are the answers that the latest effective interpretation, consistently sensi-

[1] Christopher Marlowe, *The Tragical History of the Life and Death of Doctor Faustus,* ed. John D. Jump, The Revels Plays (Cambridge, Mass., 1962, rptd. 1965), v.83. I cite this edition everywhere but in those places where I have occasion to refer to W. W. Greg's A and B texts in his *Marlowe's Doctor Faustus 1604–1616: Parallel Texts* (Oxford, 1950).

tive to the ambiguities "woven into the entire dramatic fabric" of the play, must begin by remarking the severe "critical discord" among contemporary interpretations.[2] Still problematical in its date, its textual bibliography and authorship, and in its biographical and historical bearings, Marlowe's show, like Mephostophilis', remains equally problematical in its meaning. The dancing devils mean something more than "nothing," after all, since they help to seduce Faustus into handing over the copy of his pact with Lucifer (v.88). Interpretive speculation means something, too, for almost all of it tends to assert either heterodox meanings or orthodox meanings of the show. Some interpretations, however, assert its underlying ambiguity and thus assert that the show is at least not orthodox. But some orthodox interpretations, if sufficiently open to certain ambiguities, imply that things may be in doubt.

Interpretation must speculate beyond "slender questions Wagner can decide," for even the Prologue and the Epilogue, spoken from outside the dramatic fiction, generate ambiguities. In the Prologue, for example, there is the sexual confusion of a Muse which vaunts "*his* heavenly verse" (6), thus anticipating Helen's later assimilation to Jupiter and Apollo, and Faustus' to Semele and Arethusa, and to Diana, too. And if "heavenly" reverberates ironically almost everywhere in the play, as Mizener

[2] Since I cite some eighty studies of Marlowe's play, I have listed their full references in a bibliographical appendix to this essay. I cite these studies with the authors' names and with numerals indicating the appropriate page numbers. Multiple studies by the same author are distinguished one from another by the year of publication. The instant quotations in the text are from Sanders, 1968, 215 and 207. Quotations from Sanders are used by permission of Cambridge University Press.

and Heilman and others have shown, perhaps its ironies begin here. If so, the "verse"—the play—is as hellish as heavenly. The Prologue continues: "Only this, gentles—we must perform/ The form of Faustus' fortunes, good or bad" (7–8). This, the first sounding of the hero's name, perhaps glances ironically at its etymology in *faustus*, or "well-omened, fortunate, lucky," as Levin and Kocher have suggested, if for no reason other than the explicit ambiguity in "good *or* bad." The witches in *Macbeth* sing similarly of a battle that is "lost *and* won" in a play whose hero's butchery taints his "milk of human kindness." The Prologue then coalesces Faustus' academic commencement with the "good or bad" commencement of the dramatic action proper:

> So much he profits in divinity,
> The fruitful plot of scholarism grac'd,
> That shortly he was grac'd with doctor's name,
> Excelling all, and sweetly can dispute
> In th' heavenly matters of theology;
> Till, swollen with cunning of a self-conceit,
> His waxen wings did mount above his reach,
> And, melting, heavens conspir'd his overthrow;
> For, falling to a devilish exercise,
> And glutted now with learning's golden gifts,
> He surfeits upon cursed necromancy; . . .   (15–25)

There are many difficulties here. The longer we speculate upon the grace notes, the more ironic they become. "Cunning" and "conceit," because they are "at a semantic cross-roads" (Gill, xxi), import both honorific and pejorative connotations. The time sequence as the cause of the "overthrow," usually thought to refer to the end of the play, remains equivocal. If, for example, the heavens conspired Faustus' overthrow, they seem to have thrown him into the devilish exercise in the first instance. And is the exercise causal for the necromancy? If so, the heavens conspired Faustus' first step into abjuration and from thence into necromancy. And if so, the Prologue qualifies those interpretations which insist on the orthodoxy of the show and which hunt Faustus down in his *hamartia*.[3] Besides, Mephostophilis will later claim responsibility for abusing Faustus to damn him, for turning the pages of scripture in the moment of Faustus' decision to abjure divinity (xix.92–98). "Jehovah's name/ Forward and backward anagrammatiz'd" (iii.9) seems an emblem for this persistently mixed thing, its center nowhere, its circumferences everywhere, like heaven, like hell. Stretching "as far as doth the mind of man," the play enacts an oxymoron, both keen and comic, and above all memorable.

I

Because *Doctor Faustus*, like Marlowe's other plays, dramatizes "complementary aspects of . . . experience" with "multiplicity of

[3] The A-text version of line 20 is "And melting heauens conspirde his ouerthrow." The B-text version is "And melting, heauens conspir'd his ouer-throw." The Revels Plays punctuation is the editor's. The three versions vary the causal relations among Faustus' aspirations in mounting above his reach, the failure of his aspirations in the melting of his wings, and the heavenly conspiracy. There is no need here to sort out all the possible relations, but if, for example, Faustus' wings mounted above his reach and melted, the *failure* of his aspirations seems to *cause* the heavenly conspiracy. Orthodox interpretations too infrequently acknowledge the problem represented by a conspiratorial heaven. See Brooke (1952, 671) for a

vision," in Eugene Waith's comprehensive formula (1965, 229), interpretation tends toward antithesis and dispute. Thus the play is "one of the most fascinatingly ambiguous plays ever written" and imitates the "ambiguities of the human predicament" (Brooke, 1966, 101–2); it has an "ambivalent effect" (Knights, 94); it forces upon the critic a dilemma: "to haul the Devil out of Hell onto the Promethean rock, or to plunge aspiring minds into Hell" (Morgan, 24).[4] Remarking Faustus' "diabolic apotheosis," Wilbur Sanders explains the origin of the dilemma: "What we have in fact is two dramas: (1) the moralized battle for Faustus' soul—a constricting framework within which, nevertheless, most of the play operates comfortably . . . [and] (2) a tragedy of a divided consciousness in which the human is not restricted in the interests of the superhuman, but the superhuman finds its validation, if anywhere, in the human" (1964, 90–91). This is another way of saying with Levin that in Faustus' apostrophe to Helen, for example, "aesthetic rapture is framed by the ethical situation" (1964, 28–29), or that Marlowe occasionally glances beyond the dogmatic framework (1952, 134).

Yet doctrine and theology more than drama and spectacle attract contemporary interpretation. Even a critic who thinks that "no doctrinal analysis is possible" (because the play is a play and not the cultural document or "significance" Levin and

---

heterodox acknowledgment tempered with a warning that the line is merely conventional.

[4] Four recent popular editions exactly replicate the dilemma; one teaches the heterodox reading (Ribner, 1963), one the orthodox (Kirschbaum, 1962), and two commit themselves neither way (Jump, Gill).

M. M. Mahood and others are said to make of it) can yet declare
Marlowe's "moral purpose . . . an evil one" (Steane, 62, 154). On
the other hand, the play dramatizes "Evangelical Reform doctrines" (Davidson, 514 ff.), and "no more obvious Christian
document [exists] in all Elizabethan drama" (Kirschbaum, 1943,
229). It is not an "obvious Christian document," however, because "Christianity has few positives in this play" (Gill, xxvii);
still, it demonstrates an offense against a "divinely established
hierarchical order," and its "moral framework . . . is the orthodox
Christian Scheme" (Duthie, 84–85); but it is also "essentially
anti-Christian" and mirrors "agnostic intellectual confusion"
(Ribner, 1962, 110; Ribner, 1963, xxxviii). The line of contradiction stretches out to the crack of Faustus' doom,[5] but it begins in the play as well as in the variety of critical and scholarly
approaches to it. When Levin, for example, explicated the Epi-
cureanism and Atheism in the play, Battenhouse reproved him for
failing to be shocked by these heresies, "anathema," as he had
said earlier, "to every Elizabethan" (1953, 533; 1941, 7). But one
man's anathema, whether in our time or in Marlowe's, is another
man's art. If novelty of theology or morality were unknown in

[5] There are many other examples: its "orthodoxy is unimpeach-
able" (Speaight, 36); although it derives from "Christian theological formulations," it fails to dramatize "the Christian view of suffering in its entirety" (Cole, 263–64). Judged from Christian traditions
on the pagan classics alluded to in the play, it is "completely orthodox" (McAlindon, 222–23). Marlowe's "affirmation" may be "specifically Christian," but the "play as a whole" remains "a challenge
or query" (Tomlinson, 69–70). Among some twenty-four essays
published in the last twenty years, opinion divides about equally
between those who see the play as orthodox and those who see it as
heterodox or ambiguous.

Marlowe's time, De La Primaudaye's *French Academy* could not have certified that "at this day, we see nothing but contrarieties of opinions and uncertainties" (quoted in Brockbank, 22). Philip de Mornay would not have written a six-hundred-page refutation of detailed heresies in his defense of the trueness of the Christian religion. In the very year of Marlowe's birth, some Cambridge students would not have attempted to entertain Queen Elizabeth with "a blasphemous parody of the Mass that made [her] . . . enter her chamber using strong language."[6] Nor in our own time would the historical researches by Tillyard, Lily B. Campbell, and Hardin Craig, for example, have needed redress by those of Theodore Spencer, E. W. Talbert, and Roland Frye. We continue to discover that all is not one but many, and that even if it were, a play need not stand in a one-to-one relationship with its context, whether we consider the context univocal or multiple. "Contrarieties of opinions" forestall the hegemony of one or another dogma whether in Marlowe's time or in ours, and possibly nowhere more than in contemporary interpretations of *Doctor Faustus*.

These interpretations do not often make their aesthetic assumptions explicit, especially as to the relation between mimesis and idea. They merely assume such a relation, however they evaluate the supposed doctrine in the play. Similarly, when Faustus himself becomes an object of evaluation, the interpretations indulge a kind of character-mongering, without making explicit the theory of dramatic literature that warrants their doing

[6] See Marion Jones, "The Court and the Dramatists," in *Elizabethan Theatre*, ed. John Russell Brown and Bernard Harris, Stratford-upon-Avon Studies 9 (London, 1966), p. 177.

so.[7] And, again, views of Faustus diverge as sharply as views of
doctrine. He is said to be an object of derision from the very
first; he is a sensualist, he is damnable because he could have made
a salutary choice and didn't, he is insolent and stupid, he confuses
the proper relations among Will, Understanding, and Appetite,
and he thus violates the world order as defined by Tillyard
(Duthie, 84–93). He has no excuse for his sin, no special passion,
no mitigating ignorance, and his intellectual aspirations evince
sinful curiosity (J. Smith, 40; McCullen, 6–7). But he is indeed
ignorant, and in the light of 1 Timothy 1:13—"But therefore I
have obtained the mercy of God, because being ignorant I acted
in unbelief"—his ignorance mitigates his sin and saves him from
damnation (Morgan, 28). He enjoys legitimate aspirations common to all men (Sewall, 64), but if he aspires to relieve the op-
pressed under the Prince of Parma and to clothe the students in
silk, he must be harboring evil ambitions to subvert principles of
hierarchy (Duthie, 83). Admired for refusing the dagger of despair, he anyway commits "symbolic suicide" in the Helen episode (Sachs, 639). He can be defended, however, as a seeker
whose quest may be blasphemous but full of "impressive daring

[7] But perhaps we should not expect practical criticism to argue
fully the theory of literature on which it proceeds. Brooke's attempt
to fend off character-mongering in *Doctor Faustus* criticism is ex-
ceptional but obviously brief: "It is scarcely surprising that attempts
to fix [the play's] . . . attitude by analyzing its moral arguments are
not more successful than earlier efforts to find its significance in the
character of Faustus; it doesn't have an argument, and Faustus
doesn't have a character. The play is an outstandingly full realization of the . . . particular form" (1966, 101–2).

and intellect," as a "martyr . . . for a great cause"—the "enlargement of human power" (Bevington, 255), and, endowed with Marlowe's eloquence, as an embodiment of "sweetness with power and power with sweetness in a way that disarms conventional moral judgments" (Brockbank, 33–34). Assuming Faustus' salvation at the end, Morgan wryly warns critics that in consigning Faustus to damnation they practice "more than heavenly power permits" (29). But Morgan's warning is a cry in a wilderness of interpretive judgment.[8] Just as there seem to be two plays dramatizing different doctrines, there seem to be two Faustuses, the form of his critical fortunes, like his dramatic fortunes, "good or bad."

Critical interpretation of certain recurrent and strictly literary topics also divides in controversy. Interpretation assumes, for example, that the play is a tragedy, but it rarely makes its conception of tragedy explicit. Michel, who has most cogently and persuasively denied the possibility of Christian tragedy, tests the

[8] Other representative condemnations of Faustus insist, for example, that he is guilty of usurpation upon the devil (Gardner, citing John Donne, 324, n.11), of "usurpation upon deity" (Frye, 323), and of sinful "curiosity" as defined in the patristic tradition (Maxwell, 1947, 51; J. Smith, 40); he is also guilty of "sloth" (Hawkins, 202), and he suffers from "carnal security" and "sinful complacency" in citing the story of the thief upon the cross (Sachs, 639). In Heilman's notably sensitive but finally one-sided study of the play's texture and nuances, Faustus becomes a positivist intellectual who secularizes eternity, rejects knowledge as knowledge unless it is useful, and falls into the error of "wanting science to do the work of philosophy and religion" (317, 319, 326).

play with his touchstones for tragedy and finds that it "disinte-
grates under the incompatibility of [its] . . . ingredients" (231).
Sewall, on the other hand, thinks it the first "Christian tragedy,"
though its world is "not comfortable or secure" but tragic precisely because it does not "establish . . . moral truth" and because
it escapes judgment by the "orthodox world" (57–58). Interpretive debate on *Doctor Faustus* as tragedy thus circles back to
doctrine, the critics apparently unable to follow Helen Gardner
in her caveat that the "unity of tragedy is destroyed if the critic
makes himself either the champion of the hero or the advocate
of Eternal Law" (335). Wilbur Sanders, a prominent exception
to such championship, locates Faustus' tragic agon not on a bat-
tleground of conflicting and external moral traditions but in the
particularities of Faustus' torment, "his immovable conviction
and irresistible doubt." Sanders concludes, however, that the play
as a whole moves only intermittently in a "region of tragic potential" (1964, 87–88). Although Helen Gardner and Sewall
have faced this extraordinarily complex topic most directly, the
nature of the tragedy will probably continue to stimulate interpretation. To dismiss the tragedy seems a formidable task, however, for the form of Faustus' fortunes follows a clearly tragic
curve from ambiguous decision to ambiguous death, from mystery to mystery. The nodes of the curve are familiar enough;
heroic self-sufficiency and tragic self-confidence, decision as
dilemma, choice, consequences, suffering, tardy transvaluation,
and death felt as loss, all these deeply cross-purposed by good
and evil as defined by Faustus' conflicting beliefs and doubts.
The extent to which the play is tragic in these terms is the extent

to which it is not Christian, if Christianity in dramatic mimesis must be a divine comedy of redemption history.[9]

Other controversial topics in interpretation of the play as dramatic literature are the morality elements, the plot structure, the comic episodes and ingredients, and the verse as a test of doctrine.

Almost all writers on the morality elements sense the inconsistency between the allegorical tradition behind the elements and the deallegorized or particularized tragical history of a Faustus who transcends that tradition. And almost all evince some slight discomfort in trying to account for the transcend-

[9] Michel's beautifully evocative essay denies the possibility of Christian tragedy and should stimulate further efforts to interpret the relation between doctrine and tragedy in *Doctor Faustus*. Perhaps Mr. Michel himself will elaborate the "incompatibility" he speaks of. On this general issue see Sylvan Barnet, "Some Limitations of a Christian Approach to Shakespeare," *ELH*, XXII (1955), 81–92. A. P. Rossiter's "Shakespearian Tragedy," part of his *Angel with Horns* (London, 1961, rptd. in Michel and Sewall, 181 ff.), Helen Gardner's discussion of the topos of the "fortunate fall" (320 ff.), Levin's discussion of Marlovian tragedy in general (1952, 161–62), and Battenhouse's essay-review of Levin's *Overreacher* (1953, 541–42) usefully specify some of the terms that need attention. (The recurrence of Harry Levin's name in my text and notes records a debt for which gratitude hardly suffices. *The Overreacher* [1952], a truly seminal work, has been glossed both in large and in small by almost all succeeding interpretations of Marlowe and *Doctor Faustus*.) Mizener, Heilman, Ribner (1962), Cole, Steane, Bradbrook (1935, 1964), Brooke (1952), Heller, and Frye, among others, address themselves to the nature of the tragedy, sometimes incidentally, but they come to rest in positions that seem to me overly schematic.

ence and for Marlowe's reversion to an apparently outmoded
dramatic form. Brooke, for example, thinks that Marlowe uses
the "musty genre" of the morality "perversely to invert . . . its
normal intention" (1952, 669). For Brooke the "order of God"
in the play is the "order of servitude," and the play thus becomes
thoroughly subversive (1952, *passim*); the morality idea proves
untenable under Marlowe's aesthetic exploitation of the secular
potentialities in the form (1966, 103). Steane rebuts Brooke by
claiming that the morality genre offers Marlowe merely a way
to "externalize Faustus' struggle" (367). Levin considers the
morality elements materializations of Faustus' inner hell (1952,
131). Ornstein thinks that Marlowe does not use "the Morality
framework" as a "literary, 'mythical' apparatus" (172). Here, I
think, Ornstein errs but comes suggestively close to liberating
interpretation of the morality elements from some of the more
diversionary doctrinal debates. With a form traditionally committed to the highest Christian *utile* and therefore not tragic,
Marlowe shaped an apparatus for the highest tragic *dulce*.

Although Faustus' dramatic relations with the Angels, the
Seven Deadly Sins, and the Old Man have received detailed attention, interpretation has yet consistently to attend to dramaturgy and spectacle, as Wilbur Sanders does, for example, in his
remarks about the Angels' visitation in scene v. The Angels, he
says, are "abstractions, belonging to no specific time and place"
and thus are "sufficiently unindividualized to be functions of
Faustus' conscience, and sufficiently removed from the sphere of
dramatic action to symbolize an order outside of it":

Bad Angel. Go forward, Faustus, in that famous art.
Good Angel. Sweet Faustus, leave that execrable art.

Faustus. Contrition, prayer, repentance, what of these?
Good Angel. O, they are means to bring thee unto heaven.
Bad Angel. Rather illusions, fruits of lunacy,
     That make men foolish that do use them most.
Good Angel. Sweet Faustus, think of heaven and heavenly things.
Bad Angel. No, Faustus, think of honour and of wealth.

                                        Exeunt Angels.
Faustus. Wealth! . . .   (v.15–23)

Of the spectacle and dramaturgy in this apparently arid morality
moment, Sanders writes brilliantly and incisively:

> Far from being clumsily primitive, this is an immensely dra-
> matic procedure. The first effect of the interruption is to
> arrest all action on the stage, and to focus attention on the
> protagonist, suspended in the act of choice. Not until he
> speaks do we know to which voice he has been attending. It
> is the act of choice in slow motion, a dramatization of his
> strained attention to the faint voices of unconscious judg-
> ment. At the same time, his unawareness of the Angels'
> presence has the effect of revealing his blindness to the real
> issues at stake—what he takes to be a decision between con-
> trition and wealth, the forms in which the Angels' exhorta-
> tions have crystallized in his mind, is a primal decision be-
> tween good and evil. And his unconscious echoing of their
> words is a parable of his inability to evade moral categories.
> The course of self-gratification on which he is embarked is
> no more his own than are the Angels; yet it is, by the
> same token, as *much* his own as they are. He is an involun-
> tary participant in the moral order, yet he shapes the moral
> order by his action. (1968, 217)

Sanders' subtle and relatively unusual attention to spectacle profitably underscores even in the supposedly orthodox morality elements those inherent contradictions which elude dogmatic interpretations. There are many such moments of spectacle among the morality elements, and some of them, when compared with the equivalent moments in the source, contribute to the ambiguities of the play. The source, for example, prints the words of the diabolic compact in a chapter whose heading is *"How Doctor Faustus set his blood in a saucer on warme ashes, and writ as followeth"* (Jump, 126). From this hint Marlowe develops the spectacle of Mephostophilis' hasty exit when Faustus' blood congeals: "I'll fetch thee fire to dissolve it straight" (v.63). Faustus soliloquizes a claim to controlling his destiny: "Is not thy soul thine own?" (v.68). Then *"Enter* MEPHOSTOPHILIS *with the chafer of fire"* (v.69.1). As Faustus finishes writing, Mephostophilis gloats aside, "What will I not do to obtain his soul!" (v.73), while Faustus speaks: "Now will I make an end immediately. . . . *Consummatum est:* this bill is ended" (v.72, 74). The source blood does not congeal, except by implication of the chapter heading. In the play, a mysterious principle acting on Faustus' blood resists, but a countervailing principle represented in the diabolically unctuous Mephostophilis facilitates, the signing of the compact. Through the movement on the stage, the spectacle, and the property chafer, the principles contend and come to a climax when Faustus recites Christ's last words beside the gloating devil. It is impossible to believe that the Mephostophilis actor should not gesture a startled or anxious response to those words. And the whole spectacle raises questions about the ambiguous relation between the two principles. In the next moment, the contest continues but in a lower key. The hortatory legend (*"Homo fuge!"*) appears on Faustus' arm, and the spectacle subsides. Faustus persists: "Yet shall not Faustus fly" (v.81). His soul is clearly his own and just as clearly not his own. In their dramaturgy, the morality elements tragically compound rather than homiletically resolve ambiguities.[10]

Interpretations of the plot tend to construe its structure as linear or circular (or cyclical) and in turn correlative either with Faustus' triumph or with his failure. Homan, for example, perceives a linear progression toward the triumph of Faustus' heroic

---

[10] The morality elements have received their most thorough analysis in the studies by David Bevington and Douglas Cole. Bevington finds the sources for the ambivalent tensions of the *psychomachia* in certain interlude and morality patterns. The allegorical and direct representations of Faustus, and the potentially comic and actually catastrophic endings, are in conflict. Therefore "Faustus as Everyman ought to be saved, even in his final hour; yet as specific person he is damned" (261). Cole recites a host of differences between the morality tradition and Marlowe's use of it, and he emphasizes Faustus' responsibility for his own suffering as the origin of the play's tragic transcendence of the morality form (191 ff.). Homan sees the particularized Faustus as the source of the transcendence (500). Brookbank, however, harks back to ambiguities in the morality tradition itself, in its ambiguous treatment of the devil, of temptation, and of forbidden knowledge, and he thus associates these ambiguities with Marlowe's (18–19). Sewall vests the "meaning of the play" not in the morality frame but in Faustus' acting out a "mysterious tragic dynamic" (60). David Kaula contrasts the treatment of time in *Everyman* with that in *Doctor Faustus* and thus contrasts the "benevolent deity" of the morality with the "remoteness of the divine" in the tragedy (11). Palmer thinks the play no morality, because "no Vice or external mechanism" propels Faustus (1966, 26).

anagnorisis and death (503–4). Greg takes the opposite view, noting Faustus' failure, his "gradual deterioration" and "progressive fatuity" which sinks at Vanholt "to the depths of buffoonery" (1946, 97).[11] James Smith sees the plot circularly, with Faustus damned from the first and with the play a spiritual allegory that ends where it begins (48–49), and he is joined by Maxwell (1947, 49). C. L. Barber detects a "circular pattern" in Faustus' "thinking of the joys of heaven, through despairing

[11] Other examples of the analysis of structure as linear and descending may be found in Gardner (323), Frey (350–53), and Warren Smith (173). Sewall finds an ascending structure in Faustus' "new energy, new power, new command" after the signing of the pact (61). Although Levin correlates "structural weakness" with "the anticlimax of the parable" and with "the gap between the . . . bright hopes of the initial scene and the abysmal consequences of the last," he considers the plot "perfectly classical" in its five-part "climactic ascent" (1952, 124), only to be countered by Westlund for whom the mingling of the "wonderful" and the "farcical" obviates "climactic progression" (199–200). Sanders considers structural unity a mere critical invention (1964, 87–88). There are three independent studies of the linear structure. Susan Snyder shows that the play inverts the conventional seven stages of hagiography to generate a "downward career" for Faustus (566). G. K. Hunter ascribes the five-act structure he detects to the hierarchical structure of the academic disciplines; in this reading, the action moves "backwards and downwards" in a linear pattern of "increasing remoteness from first causes" (79 ff.). And Sherman Hawkins detects in the comic and middle episodes the structure of the pageant of the Seven Deadly Sins, which Faustus encounters at first only "abstractly and objectively" but must learn "concretely and intimately by actually committing them in turn" (194). Not quite structural in their interests, Beach Langston correlates part of the plot with rituals of the *ars moriendi* tradition, and Philip J. Traci permits us to construe the plot as a progress of the artist (8).

of ever possessing them, to embracing magical dominion as a blasphemous substitute" (99). In this illuminating analysis, Faustus tests a hypothesis by means of a "self-creating process . . . dramatized by tensions between what is expressed in words and what is conveyed by physical action on the stage: the hero declares what is to happen, and we watch to see whether words will become deeds" (116–17). Stimulated by Barber, we should recall that Cornelius and Valdes, and Mephostophilis, too, use the word "experience" (i.118; v.129) with the connotation of "experiment." The plot has the structure of an experiment to test, among other things, Faustus' belief that "hell's a fable" (v.128).[12] Yet Faustus believes in hell for the purpose of conjuring by "Gehenna," and the conjuring succeeds. It is an axiom of the plot, at any rate, that for "experience" to change Faustus' mind, as Mephostophilis warns him it will, Faustus must die. (But when Faustus dies, the hypothesis remains untested and the conclusion ambiguous, as I hope to show.) On the other hand, Faustus journeys to heaven and hell (viii.70) before he dies, and he suffers in addition the uncircumscribed hell that is everywhere, too, but paradoxically, for he seems to joy when he is most damnable and to suffer when most saveable, but not consistently. That is why, perhaps, in the world of the play damnable despair and saving divinity are both "base" (i.107, vi.31). Like Faustus' lines and circles, useful analyses of the plot structure should conjure the play's contradictions and Faustus' struggle with them.

A number of further studies could yet reveal significant re-

---

[12] Faustus' words seem to Brooke "one of the funniest lines in English drama" (1966, 101), since Faustus is speaking to "the devil beside him." But the words are portentous, too.

lations between plot structure and matter. If the fiction of the play assumes, for example, that necromantic power can control space and time, then the uses of space and time in the structure of the play's spectacle seem useful to consider. When Faustus, alone in the confined space of his study at the beginning, throws off the past represented in the disciplines of Galen, Aristotle, and Justinian, he hopes to control the future by imagining vast spaces to conquer. After the exposition of Faustus' aeromantic journeys to "prove cosmography" (Chorus 1.20), the spaces represented on the stage are the courts of the Pope, the Emperor, and the Duke of Vanholt and the tavern world of the subplot. In the first two courts, Faustus reverses time by rescuing Bruno and, "his fame spread forth in every land" (Chorus 2.12), by conjuring the shades of Darius and Alexander and his Paramour. The chorus points to the Emperor scenes as *examples* of Faustus' "art" (13–16). Twenty-four years later, in the Duke's court, he conjures space by building the enchanted castle in the air and fetching grapes from "countries that lie far east" (xvii.30). Just before the summons to the Duke's court, in the Horse-courser scene, the first scene after the passage of the twenty-four years, Faustus manipulates neither space nor time but himself; he confounds despair and distrust "with a quiet sleep" (xv.24), and he cites the doctrinally ambiguous story of the thief upon the cross. In one moment he has been seen defeating Benvolio's soldiers by moving trees magically across the stage, in the next, he seems wearied by the Horse-courser's bargaining and turns to rest "quiet in conceit" (xv.26). Between this moment of spiritual crisis and the last, when Lucifer brought in the pageant of the Seven Deadly Sins, almost half the play has intervened—the scenes at the papal court and at the Emperor's court, followed by the thwarted ambush. In these scenes, there have been spectacles of conflict, between the Pope and Bruno in chains and acting the footstool, between Faustus and the Roman church and its rituals and ceremonies, between Darius and Alexander in the dumbshow, and between Benvolio and Faustus. The stage has been full of noise and spectacle—Faustus kneeling under the incantation of invisibility, the procession of friars chanting the malediction, fireworks, drums, perhaps trumpets, the clash of weapons, the moving trees, Faustus' "beheading" and survival, the muddying and tearing of the Benvolio party, Benvolio's horning. The spectacles mix high and low, imperial politics and private slights, in a web of life that is of a mingled yarn. Nowhere, however, as he promises, does Faustus slay his enemies, build altars to Beelzebub, sacrifice the blood of newborn babies, burn the scriptures, slay ministers, pull down churches, or, as in the source, make himself an enemy to all Christian men. He calls for torment for the Old Man but sustains his touching friendship with the pious Scholars. And neither, of course, has he quite walled all Germany with brass. Then his life passes in the twinkling of an eye, which is how Mephostophilis brings Helen to Faustus, and he is at the "final end" (xv.22). In short, the time-structure of the plot is really in two parts—the early days of the signing of the pact and the first necromantic feats, and the last days and hours at Vanholt, with Helen, and the final scenes. Between the quiet of his sleep and the quiet of the announcement that he has been making out his will there is the mixture of the tavern episode, the hostess, the clowns, the drunks, and their incursion into the Vanholt court. Here there are no imperial conflicts, no threats to Faustus' life, no Alexander, no Darius, no Pope, no Emperor, only the grapes, the pregnant Duchess, and Faustus' harmless conjuring of the clowns into dumbness. The stage is set for a return to the dramaturgical quietude of the Old Man's appeal to Faustus, lest "sin by custom grow . . . into nature" (xviii.44), and Faustus' awed ecstasy in Helen's silent presence. If Faustus has been magically granting "the just requests of those that wish him well" (xviii.22) during the twenty-four years, we cannot help but wonder (with Boas, 216) what sin the Old Man is referring to. The Old Man's appeal ironically initiates the crisis of Faustus' attempted suicide and Helen's second appearance; the episode mirrors the ambiguity in which the reading of scripture initiates Faustus' decision to abjure divinity.

Structural interpretations regularly assume that plot somehow proves the proposition that "men are not likely to go wrong unless there is sufficient cause,"[13] that plot, the Aristotelian soul of tragedy, enacts something less problematical than an imitation of the way things are, and that tragic mystery will yield an unambiguous declaration about the origin of tragic catastrophe. Regardless of whether at the end Faustus is damned or saved (an unresolved issue, as we shall see), his pact on the one hand commits him to exactly twenty-four years of life and to a definite time of death. On the other hand, it remains a question right through Faustus' last words whether repentance can control the pact. If the plot structure is bifold, it is a structural correlative, if anything, to division, struggle, and contradiction. It achieves these metaphors in the dramaturgical but ambiguous dismember-

[13] J. V. Cunningham, *Woe or Wonder* (Denver, 1951), p. 120.

ment of Faustus' body. For Marlowe's play, assumptions about the plot structure as a cause-and-effect sequence remain arguable.

When interpretation adverts to the comic elements, it inquires whether or not the elements are intrinsic parts of the whole, and if they are, whether they disvalue Faustus or honor him, and in what ways. L. C. Knights considers intrinsic interpretations of the comic elements to have been "thought up" when seen as contrastively "presenting the gross stupidity of sin" (96). A. L. Rowse thinks the comic elements merely add to the "sensational appeal" (155). John D. Jump cautions critics against fashionably forcing the elements into relationships that do not exist (lxix-lx), and Michel Poirier, like Rowse, considers the elements designed to entertain "the less enlightened theater-goers" (136). These are decidedly minority voices. The comfortable majority, which accepts, in Levin's phrase, the "intrinsic—if not essential" (1952, 123) function of the comic and middle scenes, divides into two groups. The first, the more numerous, assumes that the comic elements disvalue Faustus in symbolizing his repudiation of "creation in favor of chaos" (Frye, 325). The second group generally, with Levin, considers the comic elements a dark background against which the overplot becomes "luminously adumbrated" (1952, 123).[14]

[14] Further examples of the first group may be found in Duthie (86–87), Hunter (90), Maxwell (1961, 165), and Westlund (200). The second group includes Ribner's opinion that if the comic elements demonstrate the paltriness of Faustus' gains, they at the same time enlarge his heroism by underscoring the correlative supineness of "Christian submission" (1963, xxxviii). Brooke extrapolates from Wagner's scene with Robin the extreme opinion that it mocks "the

No doubt the notoriously difficult problems of authorship and of textual bibliography confound interpretations of the comic elements. But if we accept the B-text as Marlowe's, or if we decide that we must deal with the B-text regardless of its authorial problems, at least two things are worth further inquiry. One is the thematic relation between the comedy and the tragedy. The first Wagner scene, for example, reminds us immediately that Faustus, who was "wont to make our schools ring with *sic probo*," has been exercising his "concise syllogisms" not only to gravel "the pastors of the German church" but to decide, as he does, that divinity is base (ii.1–2, i.107–12). Wagner, furthermore, triumphs over the Scholars in his comic use of logic. A major thematic relationship between the comic and the tragic arises in the first soliloquy, where the language of command, lordship, authority, dominion, fame, and freedom contrasts with the language of servility, service, bondage, threat, and their spiritual, intellectual, and psychological equivalents. The first two lines of Wagner's scene with Robin sound this contrast for the first time in the comic plot:

play's whole assumption and mocks conjuration, belief in devils, everything" (1966, 100). Besides studies of the comedy of evil descended from the morality tradition (Cole, Bevington) and Morgan's assimilating the entire play to a harlequinade that reduces the audience to "grinning horror and chuckling dismay" (24), four independent studies of the comic elements agree that the comedy is intrinsic but disagree as to its honorific or derogatory effect on Faustus (Warren Smith, Ornstein, Bradbrook [1962], and Crabtree). Among the latter, Crabtree has been less influential than he deserves to be. He finds the comic subplot fully unified and contrastively amplifying "Faustus' dignity" (8). He is almost alone in his enthusiastic appreciation of the comic spectacle.

Wagner. Come hither, sirrah boy.
Robin. Boy! O, disgrace to my person! Zounds, boy in
    your face! ... (iv.1–2)

Grace, person, God's wounds, a conflict over status—all are thematically relevant. It is not only, as some think, that the comedy contrasts with the tragedy but that conflict and contradiction inhere everywhere in the world of the play. The papal-court scene, for example supposedly levies on anti-Catholic bias in Marlowe's audience and dramatizes conflicts we would suppose to be unambiguous, and favorable to Bruno. But the conflict is not simple. The Pope cites a precedent for the superiority of papal authority over secular authority. But Bruno cites a countervailing precedent:

> Pope Julius swore to princely Sigismund,
> For him and the succeeding popes of Rome,
> To hold the emperors their lawful lords.

Bruno therefore claims his authority from Carolus the Fifth. But the Pope has a reply:

Pope. Pope Julius did abuse the church's rights,
    And therefore none of his decrees can stand. (viii.146–52)

Here ambiguity inheres in the very spectacle of the two popes competing with each other, claimed right encountering claimed right.

    The second thing worth further inquiry, once we overcome disintegrationist resistance to the extant B-text as a whole, is the effect of the middle episodes on our interpretation of the ending. The last of the middle episodes, which mixes drunkards, devils, and dukes at Vanholt, celebrates Faustus as "master doctor,"

susceptible of "great deserts," "so kind," deserving of "love and
kindness," the provider of "artful sport [which] drives all sad
thoughts away" (xvii, *passim*). It is useless to contemn Faustus'
"buffoonery" in the grape-conjuring as a gross lapse from the
grand imaginings of the first soliloquy. Faustus himself knows
that conjuring the grapes is "but a small matter" (xvii.19). When
the plot returns to the tragic, the Scholars fail to recriminate
Faustus for the "wonders" he has done; they do not even know
that he has sold his soul to the devil (xix, *passim*), and nothing
in their testimony suggests, as the homiletic source does, that
Faustus has led a "damnable life." If the play indeed dramatizes
orthodox doctrine, would it not, apart from successful necromancy, dramatize Faustus' unambiguous reprobation?

Just as doctrine intertwines interpretations of the tragedy,
the morality elements, the plot structure, and the comic elements,
it also proves inseparable from discussions of the supposed contrast between the superiority of the verse and prose in the great
passages and the supposed ineffectiveness of the rest, especially
in the homiletic speeches by the Good Angel, the Old Man, and
the Prologue and Epilogue. Heterodox readings speak, for example, of the "dull and feeble bleatings of the Good Angel," which
contrast with the "finest verse" opposed to "the declared Christian moral" (Brooke, 1952, 665–68).[15] Among the orthodox,
Westlund attempts to rationalize the inferiority of the Good
Angel's speeches thus: "God's infinite love and mercy are under-
played so that the burden of salvation lies upon Faustus alone";

[15] See Knights (95), Heller (60), and Steane (365–66) for corre-
lations between the doctrine and the quality of verse. If euphonic
symbolism reveals anything about doctrine, however, the revelation
is yet to come. Harry Morris' study wisely avoids the correlation
(149–54).

and the Old Man's failure to deter Faustus shows the "terrifying difficulty of repentance in the world of the play" (201–2). But spectacle, as in the episode of Faustus' congealed blood, renders damnation equally difficult. Besides, if the Good Angel speaks inferior verse, so does the Bad Angel. The quality of the poetry seems an unlikely source for resolving doctrinal ambiguity.

II

Contemporary interpretation of the foregoing topics at least acknowledges the play as dramatic literature, but very little of it helps to locate the play in the spectacle on the stage. And it is stage spectacle which furnishes Marlowe his chief means of imitation.[16] In his theater, these means are a gesturing, costumed,

[16] Some historical sources of the neglect may be observed in Havelock Ellis' introduction of the play as a "dramatic poem" (171), T. S. Eliot's interest in Marlowe's poetry for its "intensity," "style," and "tone" (100–8), and Una Ellis-Fermor's view of the play as a Renaissance document in the history of ideas. George Pierce Baker's celebration of Marlowe's "theatric effect" stimulated no careful study of Marlowe's spectacle. But more recently, Jocelyn Powell, Glynne Wickham, and John Russell Brown have begun to think of Marlowe's plays in the theater. Wickham, for example, rightly suggests that as a libretto, a Marlowe play "takes on an altogether different air in the theatre" and that the apparently bleak "comings and goings" have a "very different character *on the stage*" from their character in the printed text (193–94). Almost all other contemporary interpretations address themselves to spectacle only incidentally. See, for example, Hawkins' observations about the emblematic language of the costumes and properties in the papal-court episodes (196). *Doctor Faustus* needs attention to its spectacle of the kind accorded brilliantly and concretely to *Edward II* by Eugene Waith (1964) and to *Tamburlaine* by W. A. Armstrong.

speaking actor moving across a relatively bare platform, and
translocalizing space to generate the passage of time. To learn
more about whether and what the show means to mean, we must
imagine the play in Marlowe's theater and attend to its implicit
dramaturgy and spectacle, even though we may thus find ourselves abiding Lucifer's exhortation, "Talk not of paradise or
creation, but mark the show" (vi.110). John Russell Brown, one
of the few writers who have marked Marlowe's show, has called
our attention to Marlowe's occasional contentment with spectacle, "with [stage] action and no words at crucial moments"
(164). This seems an expression of special theatrical interests,
but it is certainly the case that in *Doctor Faustus* spectacle sustains ambiguity. Consider, for example, four moments of decisive
spectacle for their implications about what the show means, and
how.

The first is the moment of Faustus' decision to abjure divinity. It is a moment of tragic choice. For the preceding moments, we must envisage a lone figure, bearded, as we learn in
the episode of the Benvolio ambush, and wearing a doctor's robe
with surplice and cross, as we learn from Renaissance traditions
about Edward Alleyn in the part (though another tradition reports Faustus' wearing of Indian silk). "Having commenc'd" and
having decided to be a "divine in show" and "to level at the end
of every art" (i.3–4), Faustus reviews the academic disciplines.
Obviously gifted with a superior intellect, he just as obviously
suffers the torment of his powerlessness. He seeks for "greater
miracles" and pointedly contrasts the confining spaces of his
study with "whole cities" outside it. His Latin and Greek tags
emphasize his conquest of the past but his former slavery to "pal-
try legacies," to studies "servile and illiberal," and also to his

present condition: "Yet art thou still but Faustus and a man," a quintessence of dust. He resists these inhibitions and struggles to be infinite in faculties, in apprehension a god. Although concerned to explore various verbal and ritual patterns in the play, C. L. Barber yet troubles to envisage the aspiring Faustus in his study. When Faustus decides that the necromantic books are heavenly, Barber sees the actor using "gesture to express the new being which has been seized, standing up and spreading his arms as he speaks the tremendous future-tense affirmation: 'All things that move between the quiet poles/ Shall be at my command'" (117). In the moment of his decision, the stage implies a greater world of which the cloistered study represents but a fragment. We hear of provinces, wind, clouds, all nature's treasury, earth, sky, the elements, India, the ocean, orient pearl, all corners of the new-found world, Germany, the Rhine, Antwerp, Indian Moors, Spanish lords, Almain rutters, Lapland giants, Venetian argosies, and America with its golden fleece. Faustus' rhetoric of command aims to control future time: "I'll have them. . . . I'll have them. . . . I'll have them." The Prologue's strictures apart, we begin to see a conqueror play on a plane vaster than the field of Mars and the courts of kings. More will be sought for than the sweet fruition of an earthly crown. The rhetoric conflicts with the spectacle. The stage space *confines* the "studious artisan."

In this dramaturgical context, Faustus decides to abjure divinity and strives to introduce upon the stage and into his study the very eternity and the very infinity implied as spectacle in the final soliloquy. He will conquer space by freeing himself from the trap of time. But the moment of his decision is characteristically ambiguous and generates interpretive controversy:

Stipendium peccati mors est. Ha! *Stipendium, etc.* The reward of sin is death: that's hard. *Si pecasse negamus, fallimur,
et nulla est in nobis veritas.* If we say that we have no sin,
we deceive ourselves, and there's no truth in us. Why, then,
belike we must sin, and so consequently die.
Ay, we must die an everlasting death.
What doctrine call you this? *Che sarà, sarà:*
What will be, shall be! Divinity, adieu!   (i.39–47)

Interpretation here explores the state of Faustus' mind or soul,
and his mode of argument. Because the moment is his first significant choice, interpretive motive-hunting occurs here,[17] and because Faustus omits the texts for the central tenets of Christian
dogma, debate descends deafeningly. When Levin observes that
"Faustus, whether in Calvinistic or Epicurean fatalism, is anxious
to repudiate divinity and adopt necromancy" (1952, 113–14),

[17] Interpretations vary. Faustus is said to omit the texts "deliberately" (Westlund, 195), "wilfully" denying "himself the choice of
salvation," but ambiguously, since "at the end Mephostophilis will
claim to have turned the leaves and led the eyes of Faustus from
text to text" (Brockbank, 33). Steane attempts a middle position:
Faustus has "overlooked or deliberately set his face against the
text[s]," because he "has no conception of the Christian doctrine of
grace," desperate and damned as he is even before invoking the
devil (159). But if Faustus has no conception of grace, how can he
deliberately reject the conception? Astutely orthodox, James Smith
blames Faustus not for omitting the saving texts but for inventing
a divinity which denies "the basis" of "all divinity"—that is, that
"sin is of its essence voluntary" (51). Faustus' decision is a "pure
act of will" which "cannot be analyzed or understood. . . . In so far
as anything is evil, it cannot be explained by those who recognize
it as such" (52). Smith thus usefully keeps the mystery in the decision. As a struggle against deterministic time, furthermore, the
phenomenological act need entail neither good nor evil but tragedy.

Battenhouse asks, "Can it be Calvinistic? Why Calvin would have thundered those neglected texts in Faustus' ears" (1953, 538–39). Battenhouse blames Faustus for exhibiting a "vice popularly attributed to 'scholastic' education, . . . reaching for infinity with a finite Aristotelian logic" (1953, 538). But does Faustus merely chop logic here? If so, he is in company with the Good Angel, who argues tautologically: "Hadst thou affected sweet divinity,/ Hell or the devil had had no power on thee" (xix. 108–9). Levin clarifies Faustus' argument: "All men are sinners, ergo all men are mortal, he syllogizes with a sophistical shrug" (1952, 113–14). Morgan arranges the syllogism differently—All sinners are mortal, All men are sinners—and infers only two valid conclusions: All men are mortal, and Some sinners are men. When Faustus concludes that we must sin, and consequently die an everlasting, spiritual death, he utters a *non sequitur*. Thus, Morgan says, Marlowe has "ensnared his addle-pated pilgrim of the absolute in [a] diabolical . . . topsyturvydom," and "the frolic has only begun" (31–32). But granting Faustus' syllogism as the basis for his decision, two mutually exclusive doctrinal interpretations can exhaust the interpretive possibilities. In his choice, Martin Versfeld says, Faustus violates the fundamental Thomist principal of identity and thus violates the "existential logic of [salvation] history" (138). Versfeld does not need to cite the missing texts at all. Faustus sins by taking "the principle under the formality of logic, and not of metaphysics" (139).[18]

[18] A thorough theological analysis, Versfeld's essay clarifies Faustus' choice in terms very nearly phenomenological as a choice against a background of space and time. I give a brief summary of his essay, misleadingly entitled "Some Remarks on Marlowe's Faustus," and hope that it will acquire a wider audience among Marlowe critics. When Faustus bids farewell to *"on kai me on,"*

In the subtlest and clearest sustained theological exposition, Versfeld considers Faustus' choice from an orthodox perspective, but

Versfeld says, he rejects the "Aristotelian and Thomist conception
of metaphysics as the science of being, *qua* being. Now the central
principle of that metaphysic is the principle of identity, A is A."
Faustus' wish to be more than a man, when he is only a man, departs from the "nature of things" and subverts hierarchy, on which
rests the whole proof of God's existence. When Faustus assumes
that "what will be, shall be," he accepts "fatalism," by taking "the
principle [of identity] under the formality of logic and not of metaphysics. What is expressed is a timeless necessity. It is because we
have prescinded from [salvation] history, and are not working
within the existential logic of history that the possibility of redemption is excluded." Faustus therefore attempts something not even
"the omnipotence of God could bring . . . about," that is, an inversion of the Redemption so that "what was past was not past. . . .
Faustus twists [the principle of identity] . . . so as to give future
events a logical necessity. God cannot bring it about that I shall not
be damned. He has already opted for despair. Logic has annihilated
the 'time' of redemption." Hell in this view becomes "the place
where the principle of identity does not hold, and that is only another way of saying that it is no place. . . . It is simply the *absence*
of God here and now, the presence of non-being." Faustus' magic
strives for the "power of which what has been shall be, as if it were
present," that is, "to do what God cannot do. . . . Time in Augus-
tinian and Scholastic thought is existentially or concretely understood. Time is the procession of created things from and to God,
history in its full concreteness, with the Incarnation and Redemption revealing what is its ultimate metaphysical structure. The will
to misappropriate reality must therefore reveal itself as a will to
interfere with time. Philosophically this requires that we should
treat time as a logical abstraction" (137–42). Versfeld's explanation
valuably emphasizes, among other things, the monumental, even
heroic, nature of Faustus' decision in the world of the play. And it
reminds us that the decision arises from typically tragic self-confidence.

he does not *see* Faustus in the act of choosing. In a rival interpretation, Wilbur Sanders provides a rationale for Faustus' scorning the fatalism of his own argument, and he includes a dramaturgical perception of the moment. Considering the widespread Renaissance controversy over Calvinist reprobation, Sanders says that

> Faustus' syllogism is not simply a theological curiosity, nor is it a position to be rebutted and then forgotten. It has an alarming kind of internal and experiential logic which survives refutation. The predestinarian crux is the basilisk eye of Christianity. . . . Faustus is a little chirpy about [his conclusion] . . . but he immediately feels the dark compulsion of the idea: "Ay, we must die an everlasting death." It is the siren song of annihilation, inviting the guilt which is an inescapable component of personality to rise and engulf the whole being. . . . [In] that brief brooding pause we have seen his rebellion from an angle which reveals it as, in some sense, a revolt *for life*. Magic is at least one way of escaping from the gloomy pessimism of this doomed view of human existence. The essential pessimism of *Marlowe's* vision lies in the fact that magic is also, for the play, delusion. (1968, 228)

Because he does not apply to the play only one side of the controversy over the certainty of damnation on the one hand and the uncomfortably problematical nature of salvation on the other, Sanders remains dialectically true to the play in his way, as Versfeld theologically in his. Together they confirm the irreducibly complementary nature of the play.[19] In part because

[19] In the sense recently delineated for Shakespeare by Norman Rabkin, *Shakespeare and the Common Understanding* (New York and London, 1967), pp. 9–10, 19–28.

Faustus' "sense of imprisonment within the self is ... overwhelming," Sanders says, the question whether Faustus is "coerced" (by Mephostophilis, who in the B-text says that he turned the pages) "or whether he only imagines he is, is meaningless" (1968, 233). This comes close to ending debate. But with more eros, interpretation may yet become less eristic, if not in resolving all ambiguities then in tolerating them. And with more perception of the spectacle of Faustus' gestures, of his speech inflections, of his pauses, we may appreciate that the play insists on such tolerance. Observing the actor's pause, Sanders sees the ambiguity of Faustus' decision. It is not *only* a choice of death, as orthodox exegesis would have it.

One form of such tolerance is once again to imagine the solitary student in his soliloquy on the stage. How does he speak the line, "What will be, shall be"? Surely he is not merely translating the Italian proverb. Recalling Levin's allusion to "fatalism," we can say on the one hand that Faustus heroically—or foolishly —*determines* to go forward in his "damned art." But there is another way to read the line. "*Scorning* the fatality of 'What will be, shall be,'" Cole says, Faustus "performs his own act of will, and it is one of the developing ironies of the play that what he wills to be shall be" (italics added; 198). In the context of the entire speech, the scorn Cole hears in the line seems to me correct. Scorn fits the rhetoric of rejection used in the review of the other academic disciplines. The actor can easily dismiss the inevitable in contemptuous utterance and gesture: "What doctrine call you *this*?" And Faustus knows very well what he omits from scripture in his disbelief. Romans 6:23 continues: "but the gift of God is eternal life through Jesus Christ our Lord"; and 1 John 1:8, which he has read, is followed by "If we confess our sins, he is faithful and just to forgive us our sins, and to cleanse us from all unrighteousness" (1:9). Both texts enmesh the sinner in past events in a world he never made. But both texts also free him. Faustus refuses the trap of the past, and when he rejects divinity, he rejects a future determined by the past, just as Barabas rejects a similarly deterministic principle: "Were all in general cast away for sin,/ Shall I be tried by their transgression?" (*Jew of Malta*, 1.ii.115–16). The first three academic disciplines, as Faustus sees them, are indeed illiberal. So with divinity; it inhibits, and it is, again as Faustus sees it, "certainly a revolting doctrine" (James Smith, 51), "a distasteful yet ineluctable morality" (Gill, xxvii). Faustus strikes for freedom from "what shall be." To "be . . . on earth as Jove is in the sky" (i.75) requires the casting off of shackles. Doctrine apart, it is the inhibition Faustus casts away. The spectacle is the spectacle of a figure whose gestures reject containment, a figure which does not know how to die to the world; his sense of space and time transcends particular theologies in the theater, though the terms he uses are Christian. Divinity in the moment of his choice means phenomenological restraint. As he struggles between divinity and magic, and chooses magic, the prospect he opens is the "four-and-twenty years of liberty" (viii.61) he later calls it. But only twenty-four years.

In the moment when Faustus prays and Lucifer answers, another moment of choice compounds ambiguity of doctrine with ambiguity of spectacle. Faustus curses Mephostophilis for refusing to tell him who "made the world"; Mephostophilis enjoins him, consistently enough, to "think . . . of hell"; but Faustus himself turns to the creation: "Think, Faustus, upon God, that made the world"; Mephostophilis exits threatening: "Remember this!" Faustus, now alone, wonders whether it is not too late for repentance; the two Angels enter to urge both the uselessness and the effectiveness of repentance, and "*Exeunt* Angels." Faustus, again alone, prays: "O Christ, my saviour, my saviour,/ Help to save distressed Faustus' soul," but Lucifer enters and answers, "Christ cannot save thy soul, for he is just;/ There's none but I have interest in the same" (vi.69–88). An obvious dramaturgical option for actors and directors, the duration between the prayer and the entrance raises significant questions even before Lucifer speaks and even if with Helen Gardner we think it "hateful that in tragedy Eternal Law should argue" (335). But if official repentance requires prayer, why is it Lucifer who answers that "Christ *cannot* save" Faustus? And what means *this* show? That Faustus, as some think, has damned himself from the moment he abjured God?

Orthodox interpretation tends to minimize or rationalize this spectacular challenge to orthodoxy.[20] Because Faustus is alive,

[20] Some interpretations note the moment of Lucifer's entrance but not its ironic ambiguities. M. M. Mahood, for example, sees the moment as a formal feature of plot structure; with Faustus "on the verge of recovery in his cry," the "moment represents a true *peripeteia*; no divine messenger, but . . . Lucifer appears to derive all thought of salvation out of the hero's mind (71–72). Similarly, Sachs sees the moment as a moment of dramatic suspense "in a situation that by its nature cannot be suspenseful, since Faustus' despair . . . [renders] his reprobation a foregone conclusion" (638). Kirschbaum notices merely Lucifer's "prodding" of Faustus (1943, 237). Greg says only that Lucifer's recitation of Christ's justice shows "admirable logic" (this, because having already become a spirit

James Smith says, he hopes and prays, but because he is spiritu-
ally dead, he has no hope, thus Lucifer's entrance (47–48).
McCullen thinks the prayer a "saving step in the right direction"
but an ineffective one because Faustus is incapable of claiming
the "offered grace" (14). But, we may ask, hasn't Faustus claimed
it in his prayer? And is it not odd that Lucifer should cite Christ's
retributive justice here? What redemption call you this? If anything, the dramatic situation suggests that Lucifer should taunt
Faustus for lacking grace. Levin perceives the moment differently and dramaturgically: "Faustus, prompted by the Good
Angel for the nonce, inevitably breaks down and calls upon
Christ. Thereupon—most terrifying shock of all—it is Lucifer
who rises with Beelzebub, presumably through the trap from
below the stage, to hold Faustus to the letter of their agreement"
(1952, 129). Faustus prays, however, not because of the prompt-
ing, or not only because of it, but because of his own thought of
God earlier. He seems, indeed, not to hear the Angels at all. From
wondering whether it is not too late, he moves directly to his
prayer to Christ, while the Angels enact the deep divisions within

when he signed the pact, Faustus is damned [1946, 99]). Westlund
thinks the moment dramatizes Faustus' limitations and the "supremacy of divine over infernal powers [which] lead him to think of
God and call for Christ" (199), but he explains neither Lucifer's
supremacy over the prayer nor Faustus' independently thinking of
God in the first instance. Cole appreciates the prayer as an attempt
to resolve conflict but explains the attempt away: Faustus' "relationship with the devil has undergone a change to counter the new
tendency in his character" (213). Perceptively arguing the "bi-fold
authority" in the play and seeing the moment as a "climax of balance" in which Faustus learns "what damnation is," Mizener almost
renders the irony explicit (86–88).

him. The moment is indeed terrifying—and troubling. It ought
to unsettle orthodox interpretations more than it does. Faustus
submits to Christ only to receive an inexplicable rebuff. Or is it
only that, somehow faster than Christ, Lucifer, like Mephostophilis before him, hastens to "enlarge his kingdom" (v.40)?
Mephostophilis, however, has earlier supplied the ground rules
for hastening "*per accidens* . . . when we hear one rack the name
of God,/ Abjure the scriptures and his saviour Christ" (iii.48,
50)—which is exactly the opposite of what Faustus has done in
his prayer to Christ. The heavenly prayer thus infernally answered enacts another oxymoron. Although Faustus has invoked
the texts missing from his syllogism earlier, he has failed, or they
have failed him. The ambiguity renders judgment impossible,
for from one point of view Faustus has bravely struggled against
the threat of being torn to pieces, but from another he has
weakly succumbed to the divinity he earlier dismissed so scorn-
fully. Another aspect of the oxymoron here is his belief that he
has repented, for he thinks the diabolic threat is about to be carried out: "O Faustus, they are come to fetch thy soul" (vi.92).
And still another is his apparent belief that his repentance will
cause his immediate death—orthodoxy would find the belief damnable—although the infernal trinity does not enact the threat.
So from the infernal point of view, Faustus has not repented.
But because he has not been torn to pieces, either, the Good
Angel's words seem the more trustworthy: "Repent, and they
shall never raze thy skin" (vi.84). The moment is ironic, finally,
in that Faustus' repentant prayer and its result confirm him in his
presumptuous despair, for Lucifer's entrance seems to show that
Christ cannot indeed save Faustus' soul. The harder we look at

this moment, the more troubling it becomes. As part of the spectacle, the pause between the heavenly prayer and Lucifer's infernal entrance, perhaps just as Faustus is crossing himself, contains a striking ambiguity, which doctrine cannot easily resolve. The pause and the prayer are Marlowe's inventions and do not appear in the source. In this moment, Faustus' accusation that Mephostophilis "has . . . damn'd distressed Faustus' soul" is both true and false. Mephostophilis, if his doctrine is good doctrine, came, after all, *"per accidens,"* but Faustus, after all, abjured divinity. Lucifer's remark proves also both true and false: "Christ cannot save thy soul, for he is just" (vi.87). Paradox, perplexity, and, once again, Faustus' struggle with phenomenal space and time inhere in impressive spectacle. The Angels have given contradictory answers to Faustus' question, "Is't not too late?" (vi.80). And the offstage spaces of heaven and hell mix inextricably. Hell has become phenomenally and terrifyingly close, and all too rapid in its operations. Heaven seems too remote, hell, too near. The stage platform now seems in motion toward the ubiquitous hell Faustus has been instructed in. Though heaven's emissary in the Good Angel still seems seductively powerful enough to urge prayer upon Faustus and to collaborate with his own thoughts of "God, that made the world," heaven seems increasingly powerless, and the world of the stage becomes an arena for Faustus' torment, even when he abides Christ's way, and prays.

Contemporary interpretation has thoroughly explored for its doctrine and its verse the moment of Faustus' decision to achieve Helen. But the spatial context of its spectacle deserves exploration, too. To appreciate this context, we must briefly

review the spatial uses of the stage and the theater in the interim
between Faustus' infernally answered prayer to Christ and his
evocation of Helen. Following Faustus' terrified vow "never to
look to heaven" (vi.98), Beelzebub invites him to "sit down"
(vi.105) for the pageant of the Seven Deadly Sins, during which
Envy exits on the speech, "But must thou sit and I stand? Come
down, with a vengeance!" (vi.135). This implies that Faustus
and the devils observe the pageant from the "state" later made
explicit in the scenes at the papal court and the Emperor's court.
"Come down" implies that the "state" is probably on a dais. In
the papal court, Bruno protests his being forced to play footstool
to the Pope mounting the "state pontifical": "Proud Lucifer, that
state belongs to me:/ But thus I fall to Peter, not to thee"
(viii.93–94). This spectacle, I conjecture, foreshadows the spectacle of the final soliloquy. In the Emperor's court, the Emperor
views the dumbshow of Alexander and his Paramour and, *"leaving his state, offers to embrace them, which* FAUSTUS *seeing suddenly stays him"* (xii.54.5–6). So Faustus briefly shares the state
but not, as in the slapstick of the Roman scenes, subversively.
After the episode of Benvolio's horning and ambush, the play is
three-fourths over, twenty-four years pass, and Faustus in the
Horse-courser episode sleeps his distrust away as the "final end"
approaches (xv.22). Helen "passeth over the stage" in her two
appearances, and if Allardyce Nicoll is correct,[21] she passes from
the theater yard up to the platform and back down to the yard.
Hell, in short, begins to encroach upon the theater itself, for if
Helen is a succuba, as Greg suggests, she begins and ends her
progress in hell.

[21] "Passing over the Stage," *ShS*, XII (1959), 47–55.

The Helen scene deeply divides contemporary interpretation. Greg insists (1946) that in it Faustus commits the sin of demoniality, but Brooke insists that the demoniality is shadowy, because Faustus' "moral assertion" renders "the theological . . . as trivial as it was meant to be" (1952, 683–84). In the source, the episodes of the Old Man's first encounter with Faustus and of Faustus' making Helen his concubine are disjunct in time. Marlowe collocates the second entrance of the silent Old Man with Helen's silent passage over the stage and thus dramatizes decision as spectacle, as in Faustus' decision to conjure and in his prayer to Christ. Given the spectacle of the two silent figures, doctrinal considerations aside, Faustus now seems, however, to have no real choice. The Old Man enters as Faustus speaks the line, "And all is dross that is not Helena" (xviii.105). When Faustus continues his famous apostrophe, perhaps glancing hesitantly at the "dross" of the Old Man, he recapitulates a past ("I will be Paris . . ."—xviii.106 ff.) gripped so eloquently in his imagination that he already imagines reenacting it in the future. The second part of the apostrophe is a secular version of ecstatic confession masked as anticipation, a truly creative evocation of the past for a fantastic project in the conquest of future time. When Faustus leaves the stage with Helen for a consummation so ambiguously to be wished, he descends with her to the yard and to the audience, which has thus taken up a cosmic vantage point from which to view the phenomenon of hell. The Old Man is attacked by the devils:

> Satan begins to sift me with his pride:
> As in *this furnace* God shall try my faith,
> My faith, vile hell, shall triumph over thee.

> Ambitious fiends, see how the *heavens* smiles
> At your repulse and laughs your *state* to scorn!
> Hence, *hell!* for hence I fly unto my God.
>
>   (italics added; xviii.122–27)

Apart from a few oblique earlier allusions to this "world" (cf.
xiv.19 and xiii.82) in typical Marlovian expansiveness, "this furnace" for the first time seems explicitly to refer to the spaces of
the theater itself, "heavens" to the conventional term for the
upper reaches of the stage, and "state" presumably to the raised
throne or dais apparently used earlier in the several court scenes.
So in "Hence, hell!" the Old Man encompasses the entire theater
and implies that the devils have entered onto the "state." His
encompassing view leaves no space in the theater for this world.
More important, his confidence in the triumphantly smiling
heavens undergoes immediate dramaturgical irony in the very
next, perhaps simultaneous, entrance, which thus implies the
spectacle of the final scenes: "*Thunder. Enter* LUCIFER, BEELZE-
BUB, *and* MEPHOSTOPHILIS [*above*]." Lucifer speaks: "Thus from
infernal Dis do we ascend/ To view the subjects of our monarchy" (xix.1–2). This speech also encompasses the entire theater and spectacularly subverts the Old Man's confidence but
confirms his location of hell in "this furnace." The infernal conclave takes its place on the "state" formerly occupied by Faustus,
the Pope, and the Emperor. (The stage direction, [*above*], is
Greg's emendation, as the similar one for scene iii, where the
devils supervise Faustus' conjuring, is Boas', but the internal
allusions to the "state" imply that in both places the devils are in
"state," with Lucifer probably seated on a throne.) Lucifer's
view of his "monarchy" also sweeps over the audience. No one

else is on the stage. Mephostophilis says, "Here in this room will wretched Faustus be" (xix.8), but here now is hell, too.

The stage is now set for the fourth moment I wish to consider, the scenes with the Scholars and the final soliloquy. Again, it is a moment of decision for Faustus, and it is ambiguous. The spatial spectacle, with Lucifer and the devils in "state," approximates to Usumcasane's vision in *2 Tamburlaine:*

> Blush, Heaven, to lose the honour of thy name!
> To see thy footstool set upon thy head! . . .
> To see the devils mount in angels' thrones,
> And angels dive into the pools of hell!
> For if he die thy glory is disgraced;
> Earth droops and says that hell in heaven is placed.
>
> (v.iii.28 ff.)

Leech says of Lucifer's ascent from Dis to the "above" that "we have here a remarkable inversion of the universe's normal order. . . . The visual effect, indeed, reinforces the ambivalence that Levin and Brockbank and others have noted in the text itself. So daring is the device that at this point the extreme view of Una Ellis-Fermor becomes harder to refute" (8). Taken together with Kocher's observation that God the Father, "who looks with tenderness on his erring children," is absent from the play, the empty throne, when it descends, amplifies the inversion; furthermore, God's absence, Kocher adds, is "in no way necessary to the plot" (118). Every allusion to the heavens (they that conspired, we recall, in the Prologue and that smiled, as the Old Man saw them) now becomes crushingly ironic: "Yet, Faustus," the Second Scholar says, "look up to heaven and remember God's mercy is

infinite" (xix.39–40). With Lucifer in "state," the spectacle calls
the Second Scholar's self-assured theology ironically into question, and, as Palmer says, it conjures "the whole creation to witness the catastrophe" and the theater audience to become a
"cosmic audience" (1964, 65–66) for the confounding of hell in
Elysium. But a cosmic vantage point cannot resolve a battle between heaven and hell. And a terrestrial vantage point in Faustus'
"room" prevents judgment of Faustus' ambiguous condition.

Focused on doctrine, interpretation divides sharply here as
everywhere.[22] The deepest division comes from Morgan's opinion that Faustus achieves salvation. And Ostrowski argues that
because Faustus is notoriously unreliable as a witness and because
the devils say nothing, only "one thing is certain. They have
taken hold of his body. But what about his soul?" (301). Derived
from direct attention to the spectacle itself, Ostrowski's opinion
that Faustus' afterlife remains a mystery has some warrant, fur-

---

[22] Faustus doesn't repent, and it's his own fault (McCullen, 13;
Kocher, 108); he repents, but it is the repentance of Cain and Judas
(Mahood, 66). He is "browbeaten by the devil and forbidden to
repent when he has really repented" (Levin, quoting Santayana,
1952, 131). He is moved not by love of God but by fear (Frye,
327); he is a "coward," a "cringing schoolboy" (Duthie, 88), and a
"cowering wretch" (Gardner, 321); he sees Christ's blood in the
firmament and thinks it would save his soul, but he uses the conditional tense in "would," and, since he is without hope, his thought
remains damnably in the subjunctive (Snyder, 377; note, however,
that in B-text line 2049, Faustus says, "One drop of blood *will* saue
me" [italics added]. He falls into "total and final despair" on the one
hand but "twists and turns to escape his fate" on the other (Wilson,
82, 84). He is "heroic" and his end "glorious" (Homan, 503); he
goes to his doom "no craven sinner but violently" (Sewall, 66–67).
See Bradbrook (1935, 154–55), Empson (206), and Brockbank (59)
for other opinions.

thermore, in the Renaissance.[23] The spectacle, at any rate, blurs
the line between heaven and hell.[24]

[23] In *A Knack to Know a Knave* a dying old bailiff, though being
carried off by devils, says in the last line of the play, "Soul, be thou
safe, and body, fly to hell" (in *A Select Collection of Old English
Plays*, ed. W. Carew Hazlitt, 14 vols. [London, 1874–76], VI, 520).
And in one Renaissance edition of Nathaniel Woodes's *Conflict of
Conscience*, the Spira-Philologus figure hangs himself and presumably goes to hell a reprobate. But in another edition, the Nuntius
at the end reports Philologus' penitential tears and presumable conversion, thus implying his salvation, though nothing else in the play
changes (as Bevington notes, 247).

[24] To appreciate the spatial spectacle we need a thorough study
of the way the ending of Marlowe's play exploits the emblematic
design of the multileveled Elizabethan stage and its referents, in the
tradition of church architecture, to the tomb, the altar, and the
throne, with its conventions of hell in the cellarage, this world with
its subjects on the platform, and its kings, both secular and divine,
on the "above," or in "state," as Lucifer is in scene xix. In the
churches where European drama begins and from which Marlowe's
stage descends, the altar subsumes the heavenly "throne" and also
the Sepulchre, for in the Eucharist, to speak sacramentally, Christ
rises from his tomb after harrowing hell. At the tomb-altar-throne,
Christ defeats Satan and death. Earlier, we recall, Faustus performed
his Black Mass (iii.21–24) and conjured Mephostophilis to *arise*
("*ipse nunc surgat . . . Mephostophilis*"), thus blasphemously echoing a familiar exhortation for Christ to arise. At the end, it is Lucifer who from infernal Dis arises. The scene deploys spectacular
emblematic analogies and contrasts. I am grateful here to George
Slover, my colleague at the University of Massachusetts at Boston,
for generously sharing with me his unpublished Indiana University
Ph.D. dissertation, "The Elizabethan Playhouse and the Tradition
of Liturgical Stage Structure" (Bloomington, 1968), to which I am
indebted for some of the points above. See also George R. Ker-
nodle's *From Art to Theatre: Form and Convention in the Renaissance* (Chicago, 1944), and his "The Open Stage: Elizabethan or
Existentialist?" *ShS*, XII (1959), 1–7.

The stage usurped by Lucifer and heaven represented fleet-
ingly by a creaking throne, we may briefly retreat from spectacle
to a homiletic handbook such as Thomas Morton's *Treatise of
Repentance* (1597) to see if Faustus repents by fulfilling its requirements for the "clime up to regeneration."[25] Impossible to
indulge here, a thorough exegetical comparison between Faustus'
words in the final scenes and Morton's doctrine would reveal on
the one hand that Faustus takes every step required. At the same
time, he variously manifests the failure to take them. Consider,
for example, the requirement of prayer, in Morton's words, "the
hearing of Gods word: [and] . . . praier, or inuocation of the
name of God." Faustus prays, and once again, as in the earlier
invocation of Christ, pauses become eloquent and prayer becomes
ambiguous. I cite both of the early texts:

> O Ile leape vp to my God: who pulles me downe?
> See see where Christs blood streames in the firmament,
> One drop   would saue my soule, halfe a drop, ah my
>   Christ,
> Ah rend not my heart for naming of my Christ,
> Yet wil I call on him, oh spare me *Lucifer*!

[25] "This way or ladder . . . hath foure steps. . . . The first step
which is to be made by this carnal man now repenting, is to get the
true knowledge of . . . how sinfull and wretched he is in himselfe
by nature, and at this present. The second step is humiliation or
contrition, wrought in him by the due consideration of his own
estate. The third, is a full purpose or resolution of mind to seeke for
grace and regeneration. The fourth and last part, is the diligent
using of the meanes appointed by God, for the obtaining of grace:
the which meanes are three in number. The first is amendment of
life: the second, the hearing of Gods word: the third is praier, or
inuocation of the name of God" (London, 1597, sig. A7v, quoted in
Kocher, 109).

Where is it now? 'tis gone:
And see where God stretcheth out his arme,
And bends his irefull browes:

(A-text, 1462–69)

O I'le leape vp to heauen: who puls me downe?
One drop of bloud will saue me;   oh my Christ,
    Rend not my heart, for naming of my Christ.
Yet will I call on him: O spare me *Lucifer.*
Where is it now? 'tis gone.
And see a threatning Arme,

an angry Brow.

(B-text, 2048–53)

Following Boas as sanctioned by Greg, most critics assume that
the dark powers here fulfill their threat to torture Faustus for
calling on Christ or forgetting his vow (vi.85–95; xviii.71–78).
Of B-text line 2049–"oh my Christ,"–Greg says, "Note that B
retains A's wholly inadequate comma at the end of this line"
(1950, 397). But neither of the early texts obviates the possibility
that it is Christ who is rending Faustus' heart now. By "inadequate" Greg intends a theological judgment that Christ could not
be torturing Faustus. But Calvin says that those in despair "do
finde no rest, from being vexed and tossed with a terrible whirle-
winde, from feeling themselues to be torne in peeces by God
being angirly bent against them" (*Institution of the Christian
Religion*, quoted in Kocher, 113). In the previous scene with the
Scholars, however, Faustus has recalled the infernal threat made
in the Helen episode: "The devil threatened to tear me in pieces
if I named God" (xix.73). Whatever rends his heart, we cannot
fault Faustus as witness to his own pain.

And whatever rends his heart, interpretation must consider

the spectacle of the Faustus actor's determination to go forward
regardless:

> Yet wil I call on him, oh spare me *Lucifer*!   (A-text, 1466)
> Yet will I call on him: O spare me *Lucifer*.   (B-text, 2051)

"The moment he calls on Lucifer," Greg says, "even the distant
vision of mercy vanishes" (n.2050–3, p. 397). We may hesitate
before Greg's authority, but is Lucifer in "O spare me *Lucifer*"
unambiguously vocative? Or is it dative, and the entire line a
prayer for Christ to spare Faustus *from* Lucifer? Or is it indeed
vocative and the first half of the line a case of words flying up
and thoughts remaining below? Whatever it is, the blood vanishes from both the early texts and from the heavens of Marlowe's
theater, or so Faustus reports. Fourteen lines later and after the
half hour has struck, Faustus prays again:

> O God
> If thou wilt not have mercy on my soul,
> Yet for Christ's sake, whose blood hath ransom'd me,
> Impose some end to my incessant pain;
> Let Faustus live in hell a thousand years,
> A hundred thousand, and at last be sav'd.   (xix.165–70)

Sinful, perhaps, in earlier speaking the conditional tense in "One
drop would save my soul, half a drop" (xix.147; cf. Snyder,
n.22), Faustus now attaches no condition whatever to the Redemption by Christ, "whose blood hath ransom'd" him, as he
says. He now believes in precisely those texts missing from his
decisive syllogism in the first soliloquy. But at the same time he
wants eternity to become finite and Redemption to work in hell.
He violates the principle of identity here at the end as at the be-

ginning. Levin considers that Faustus committed an "unpardon-
able sin, a sin against the Holy Ghost. Casuistry could have found
theological loopholes had a penitent Faustus been conceivable.
But that would have presupposed an orthodox Marlowe" (1952,
132). A penitent Faustus, however, need not imply an orthodox
Marlowe. A higher heteroxody could argue that Faustus evinces
all the steps to regeneration but paradoxically suffers damnation
anyway at the hands of a wicked or indifferent God. Neither
repentant nor reprobate, Faustus proliferates ambiguities.[26] If, as
he prays, he makes the sign of the cross, the *psychomachia* becomes spectacular, even violent. He leaps toward an unresponsive
heaven and hurls himself ineffectually against the unyielding
spatial background supervised by the silent Lucifer.

If the Faustus actor enacts a Faustus repentant but damned
regardless, he may be validating Grotowski's 1963 production,
which damned a saintly Faustus for exposing the "guilty indifference, . . . even the sin of God" (133) and which thus dissi-
pated Marlowe's complementary tensions in diabolonian dramaturgy. But the spectacle resists the resolution of ambiguity. Given

[26] Sanders, as usual, appreciates the complementary quality of this
moment: "Here the very weakness of Faustus' apprehension of
Grace—expressed in the theological commonplace—is used to dramatize his desperate clutching at it. The 'incessant pain' remains the
dominant reality, redemption the impossible end-point of eternal
torment. Prayer is no longer simply the religious extreme of the
pendulum-swing, but a reflex of agony inseparable from that agony.
The repentance and the revolt are united in a single movement of
intense feeling" (1968, 241). We should recall, however, that the
commonplace, which Faustus rejected when he decided to abjure
divinity, is no commonplace in the world of the play or in Faustus'
consciousness.

a stage wholly subsumed by hell and a theatrical heavens apparently unresponsive to Faustus' apparent repentance, the devils' entrance at exactly the moment when Faustus prays, "My God, my God! Look not so fierce on me!" (xix.187), generates still another ambiguity. Frye, however, resolves it thus: "A devil enters, and Faustus cries out against him—now seen in all the terrifying ugliness which has so long been concealed— . . . and the rest is the eternal death for which he had bargained" (327–28). Of the same entrance Sanders, keeping consistently to his complementary reading, says that "the flat either/or of heaven and hell becomes a fusion in which 'My God' may be addressed either to the Deity or to the Devils," thus balancing the "irreducible love-hate that Faustus bears toward both God and Lucifer" (1968, 242).

Even the spectacle of Faustus' torn limbs fails to resolve the ambiguities. Even though they have heard Faustus confess the source of his necromantic power, the Scholars, whose theology seems conventional enough, differ about Faustus' future:

2. *Scholar*. O, help us, heaven! See, here are Faustus' limbs,
       All torn asunder by the hand of death.
3. *Scholar*. The devils whom Faustus serv'd have torn him
       thus; . . .

                                                              (xx.6–8)

If the manner of his dying signals his ultimate fate, whether Faustus has been torn by the hand of death or has been torn by the devils implies a considerable difference. On the other hand, it may imply nothing. Nothing absolutely precludes the devils' having torn Faustus without acquiring his soul. Among Faustus' fifteen wishes, prayers, and commands in the final soliloquy is his wish to be drawn into a cloud's entrails so that when they "vomit forth into the air," as he says, his "limbs may issue from" their "smoky mouths/ So that [his] soul may but ascend to heaven" (xix.161–63). Nor does the spectacle preclude, in Barber's phrase, "corroborating physical actions" (117) at the end (by contrast with Faustus' necromantic words successfully becoming deeds earlier). These heavenly "smoky mouths" are polarized with the "jaws of hell" to which the Good Angel, for the first time agreeing with the Bad Angel, consigns Faustus. Faustus hopes to be purified in the cloudy entrails, his limbs spewed forth as a thunderstone,[27] and his soul to be saved. At the end, as Faustus speaks "O soul, be chang'd into little water drops,/ And fall into the ocean, ne'er be found," there is *"Thunder and lightning"* (xix.184.1–186). The early texts do not tell us how Faustus' dismemberment occurs. The B-text stage direction is merely *"Exeunt"* (xix.190.1); the A-text stage direction is *"Exeunt with him."* These stage directions tell us nothing about how Faustus, the devils, or the infernal conclave in "state" actually leave the stage. However Faustus dies, he leaves the stage while the clock is still striking twelve and while he is still alive, uttering his thoroughly ambiguous and often-quoted last line. Time does not have its stop, earth does not gape, the heavens do not draw Faustus up, nor for all we know does hell draw him down. Faustus' struggle with them all ends when he leaves the stage, and the rest is silence, the discovery of his limbs, and valediction:

[27] An interpretation by S. K. Heninger, *A Handbook of Renaissance Meteorology* (Durham, N.C., 1960), p. 174 (cited by Jump, n. xix.157–63).

2. *Scholar.* Well, gentlemen, though Faustus' end be such
   As every Christian heart laments to think on,
   Yet, for he was a scholar, once admir'd
   For wondrous knowledge in our German schools,
   We'll give his mangled limbs due burial;
   And all the students, cloth'd in mourning black,
   Shall wait upon his heavy funeral.   (xx.12–19)

There is nothing here about "maimed rites," as we might expect,
did the Scholars consider Faustus damned. There is only "due
burial." On the other hand, a "*Christian* heart" could lament only
a damnable end. The Scholars' return restores the spaces of this
world to the stage. The cosmic spaces give way to "this room"
again. And Lucifer, who ought to speak a diabolic boast, were
hell to receive Faustus, has kept his counsel. We are left with an
equivocal spectacle. And that may be all we know on earth and
all we need to know.

When the Epilogue, equivocal as all else, enjoins the wise
from practicing "more than heavenly power permits," it does
not condemn "wonder at unlawful things," though Faustus begins his tragic career precisely by wondering. In some interpretations, as we have seen, the play itself can become an "unlawful
thing" both in the study and upon the stage. But there are more
things in heaven and in hell than are dreamt of in dogma of any
kind. If Marlowe's play is not homiletic but dramatic, not doc-
trinaire but dialectical, not dogmatic but tragic, the spectacle
may evoke but not answer Faustus' question, "What doctrine
call you this?" If with Faustus we attempt an answer, the spectacle shows only that he has been torn to pieces by unresolved
and unresolvable terms, each term a hell, nor are we out of it

until we leave the theater to realize that the play is only a play at last, perhaps something more than "nothing but to delight the mind" but also limning for us what we had forgotten we had always known, that "these are but shadows, not substantial" (xii.55) and that fundamental ontological oxymora are not for dramatic spectacle to resolve but to show, not to mean but to be. The Epilogue permits wonder before such a spectacle, the Scholar, woe. Woe and wonder, then, for the passionate suffering of Faustus, hero of the spectacle, who asks, "What means this show?"

Bibliographical Appendix

Armstrong, William A. *Marlowe's* Tamburlaine: *The Image and the Stage*. Hull, Eng., 1966.

Baker, George P. "Dramatic Technique in Marlowe," *Essays and Studies*, IV (1913), 172–82.

Barber, C. L. " 'The form of Faustus' fortunes good or bad,' " *TDR*, VIII (Summer, 1964), 92–119.

Battenhouse, Roy W. "Marlowe Reconsidered: Some Reflections on Levin's *Overreacher*," JEGP, LII (1953), 531–42.

—— *Marlowe's Tamburlaine: A Study in Renaissance Moral Philosophy*. Nashville, 1941, rptd. 1964.

Bevington, David M. *From* Mankind *to Marlowe: Growth of Structure in the Popular Drama of Tudor England*. Cambridge, Mass., 1962.

Boas, Frederick S. *Christopher Marlowe: A Biographical and Critical Study*. Oxford, 1940.

Bradbrook, Muriel C. "The Inheritance of Christopher Marlowe," *Theology: A Monthly Review*, LXVII (July, 1964), 298–305; LXVII (August, 1964), 347–53.

—— "Marlowe's *Doctor Faustus* and the Eldritch Tradition," in *Essays on Shakespeare and Elizabethan Drama in Honor* of *Hardin Craig*, ed. Richard Hosley, pp. 55–68. Columbia, Mo., 1962.

—— *Themes and Conventions of Elizabethan Tragedy.* Cambridge, Eng., 1935, rptd. 1957.

Brockbank, J. P. *Marlowe: Dr. Faustus.* Studies in English Literature No. 6. London, 1962.

Brooke, Nicholas. "Marlowe the Dramatist," in *Elizabethan Theatre*, ed. John Russell Brown and Bernard Harris. Stratford-upon-Avon Studies 9. London, 1966.

—— "The Moral Tragedy of Doctor Faustus," *Cambridge Journal*, V (August, 1952), 662–88.

Brown, John Russell. "Marlowe and the Actors," *TDR*, VIII (Summer, 1964), 155–73.

Cole, Douglas. *Suffering and Evil in the Plays of Christopher Marlowe.* Princeton, 1962.

Crabtree, John H., Jr. "The Comedy in Marlowe's *Dr. Faustus*," *Furman Studies*, IX (November, 1961), 1–9.

Davidson, Clifford. "Doctor Faustus of Wittenberg," *SP*, LIX (1962), 514–23.

Duthie, G. I. "Some Observations on Marlowe's *Doctor Faustus*," *Archiv*, CCIII (1966), 81–96.

Eliot, T. S. *Selected Essays.* New edition. New York, 1950. Pp. 100–8.

Ellis, Havelock, ed. *Christopher Marlowe.* Mermaid Series, London, 1887, rptd. New York, 1949.

Ellis-Fermor, Una M. *Christopher Marlowe.* London, 1927.

Empson, William. *Seven Types of Ambiguity.* New York, 1931.

Frey, Leonard H. "Antithetical Balance in the Opening and Closing of *Doctor Faustus*," *MLQ*, XXIV (1963), 350–53.

Frye, Roland M. "Marlowe's *Doctor Faustus:* The Repudiation of Humanity," *South Atlantic Quarterly*, LV (July, 1956), 322–28.

Gardner, Helen. "Milton's 'Satan' and the Theme of Damnation in Elizabethan Tragedy," *Essays and Studies*, I (1948), 46–66, rptd. in *Elizabethan Drama: Modern Essays in Criticism*, ed. Ralph J. Kaufmann, pp. 320–41. New York, 1961.

Gill, Roma, ed. *Doctor Faustus.* The New Mermaids. London, 1965.

Greg, W. W. "The Damnation of Faustus," *MLR*, XLI (1946),

97–107, rptd. in *Shakespeare's Contemporaries: Modern Studies in English Renaissance Drama*, ed. Max Bluestone and Norman Rabkin, pp. 90–103. Englewood Cliffs, N. J., 1961.

Greg, W. W., ed. *Marlowe's Doctor Faustus 1604–1616: Parallel Texts*. Oxford, 1950.

Grotowski, Jerzy. "*Doctor Faustus* in Poland," trans. Richard Schechner, *TDR*, VIII (Summer, 1964), 120–33.

Hawkins, Sherman. "The Education of Faustus," *SEL*, VI (1966), 193–209.

Heilman, R. B. "The Tragedy of Knowledge: Marlowe's Treatment of Faustus," *QRL*, II (1945–46), 316–32.

Heller, Erich. "Faust's Damnation: The Morality of Knowledge," *The Listener*, LXVII (1962), 59–61, 121–23, 168–71.

Homan, Sidney R., Jr. "*Doctor Faustus*, Dekker's *Old Fortunatus*, and the Morality Plays," *MLQ*, XXVI (1965), 497–505.

Hunter, G. K. "Five-Act Structure in *Doctor Faustus*," *TDR*, VIII (Summer, 1964), 77–91.

Jump, John D., ed. *The Tragical History of the Life and Death of Doctor Faustus*. The Revels Plays. Cambridge, Mass., 1962, rptd. 1965.

Kaula, David. "Time and the Timeless in *Everyman* and *Dr. Faustus*," *CE*, XXII (1960), 9–14.

Kirschbaum, Leo. "Marlowe's Faustus: A Reconsideration," *RES*, XIX (1943), 225–41.

Kirschbaum, Leo, ed. *The Plays of Christopher Marlowe*. Cleveland and New York, 1962.

Knights, L. C. "The Strange Case of Christopher Marlowe," in *Further Explorations*, pp. 75–98. Stanford and London, 1965.

Kocher, Paul H. *Christopher Marlowe: A Study of His Thought, Learning, and Character*. Chapel Hill, N. C., 1946.

Langston, Beach. "Marlowe's *Faustus* and the *Ars Moriendi* Tradition," in *A Tribute to George Coffin Taylor*, pp. 148–67. Chapel Hill, N. C., 1952.

Leech, Clifford, ed. *Marlowe: A Collection of Critical Essays*. Twentieth Century Views. Englewood Cliffs, N. J., 1964.

Levin, Harry. "Marlowe Today," *TDR*, VIII (Summer, 1964), 22–31.

Levin, Harry. *The Overreacher: A Study of Christopher Marlowe.* Cambridge, Mass., 1952.

McAlindon, T. "Classical Mythology and Christian Tradition in Marlowe's *Doctor Faustus*," *PMLA*, LXXI (June, 1966), 214–32.

McCloskey, John C. "The Theme of Despair in Marlowe's *Faustus*," *CE*, IV (1942), 110–13.

McCullen, Joseph T. "Dr. Faustus and Renaissance Learning," *MLR*, LI (1956), 6–16.

Mahood, M. M. *Poetry and Humanism.* London, 1950.

Maxwell, J. C. "The Plays of Christopher Marlowe," in *The Age of Shakespeare*, ed. Boris Ford, pp. 154–70. London, 1955, rptd. 1961.

—— "The Sin of Faustus," *The Wind and the Rain*, IV (Summer, 1947), 49–52.

Michel, Laurence. "The Possibility of a Christian Tragedy," *Thought*, XXXI (1956), 403–28, rptd. in *Tragedy: Modern Essays in Criticism*, ed. Laurence Michel and Richard B. Sewall, pp. 210–33. Englewood Cliffs, N. J. 1963.

Mizener, Arthur. "The Tragedy of Marlowe's *Doctor Faustus*," *CE*, V (1943), 70–75, rptd. in *Shakespeare's Contemporaries: Modern Studies in English Renaissance Drama*, ed. Max Bluestone and Norman Rabkin, pp. 84–89. Englewood Cliffs, N. J., 1961.

Morgan, Gerald. "Harlequin Faustus: Marlowe's Comedy of Hell," *HAB*, XVIII (1967), 22–34.

Morris, Harry. "Marlowe's Poetry," *TDR*, VIII (Summer, 1964), 134–54.

Ornstein, Robert. "The Comic Synthesis in *Doctor Faustus*," *ELH*, XXII (1955), 165–172.

Ostrowski, Witold. "The Interplay of the Subjective and the Objective in Marlowe's *Dr. Faustus*," in *Studies in Language in Honour of Margaret Schlauch*, ed. Mieczyslaw Brahmer, Stanislaw Helsztynski, and Julian Krzyzanowski, pp. 293–305. Warsaw, 1966.

Palmer, D. J. "Elizabethan Tragic Heroes," in *Elizabethan Drama*, ed. John Russell Brown and Bernard Harris, pp. 11–28. Stratford-upon-Avon Studies 9. London, 1966.

—— "Magic and Poetry in *Doctor Faustus*," *Critical Quarterly*, VI (1964), 56–67.

Poirier, Michel. *Christopher Marlowe*. London, 1951.

Powell, Jocelyn. "Marlowe's Spectacle," *TDR*, VIII (Summer, 1964), 195–210.

Ribner, Irving. "Marlowe and the Critics," *TDR*, VIII (Summer, 1964), 211–224.

—— "Marlowe's 'Tragique Glasse,'" in *Essays on Shakespeare and Elizabethan Drama in Honor of Hardin Craig*, ed. Richard Hosley, pp. 91–114. Columbia, Mo., 1962.

Ribner, Irving, ed. *The Complete Plays of Christopher Marlowe*. New York, 1963.

Rossiter, A. P. "Shakespearian Tragedy," in *Tragedy: Modern Essays in Criticism*, ed. Laurence Michel and Richard B. Sewall, pp. 181–98. Englewood Cliffs, N. J., 1963.

Rowse, A. L. *Christopher Marlowe: A Biography*. London, 1964.

Sachs, Arieh. "The Religious Despair of Doctor Faustus," *JEGP*, LXIII (1964), 625–47.

Sanders, Wilbur. *The Dramatist and the Received Idea: Studies in the Plays of Marlowe and Shakespeare*. London, 1968.

—— "Marlowe's *Doctor Faustus*," *MCR*, No. 7 (1964), pp. 78–91.

Sewall, Richard Benson. *The Vision of Tragedy*. New Haven, 1959.

Smith, James. "Marlowe's 'Dr. Faustus,'" *Scrutiny*, VIII (1939), 36–55.

Smith, Warren D. "The Nature of Evil in *Doctor Faustus*," *MLR*, LX (1965), 171–75.

Snyder, Susan. "Marlowe's *Doctor Faustus* as an Inverted Saint's Life," *SP*, LXIII (1966), 565–77.

Speaight, Robert. "Marlowe: The Forerunner," *REL*, VII (1966), 25–41.

Steane, J. B. *Marlowe: A Critical Study*. Cambridge, Eng., 1964.

Tomlinson, T. B. *A Study of Elizabethan and Jacobean Tragedy*. London and Parkville, Victoria, Australia, 1964.

Traci, Philip J. "Marlowe's Faustus as Artist: A Suggestion About a Theme in the Play," *RenP* (1966), pp. 3–9.

Versfeld, Martin. "Some Remarks on Marlowe's Faustus," *ESA*, I (1958), 134–43.

Waith, Eugene M. "*Edward II:* The Shadow of Action," *TDR*, VIII (1964), 59–76.

—— *The Herculean Hero in Marlowe, Chapman, Shakespeare and Dryden.* New York and London, 1962.

—— "Marlowe and the Jades of Asia," *SEL*, V (1965), 229–45.

Westlund, Joseph. "The Orthodox Christian Framework of Marlowe's *Faustus*," *SEL*, III (1963), 191–205.

Wickham, Glynne. "*Exeunt to the Cave:* Notes on the Staging of Marlowe's Plays," *TDR*, VIII (Summer, 1964), 184–94.

Wilson, F. P. *Marlowe and the Early Shakespeare.* Oxford, 1953.

Daniel Seltzer

SHAKESPEARE'S TEXTS AND MODERN

PRODUCTIONS

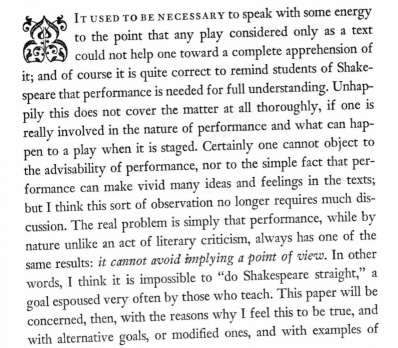

IT USED TO BE NECESSARY to speak with some energy to the point that any play considered only as a text could not help one toward a complete apprehension of it; and of course it is quite correct to remind students of Shakespeare that performance is needed for full understanding. Unhappily this does not cover the matter at all thoroughly, if one is really involved in the nature of performance and what can happen to a play when it is staged. Certainly one cannot object to the advisability of performance, nor to the simple fact that performance can make vivid many ideas and feelings in the texts; but I think this sort of observation no longer requires much discussion. The real problem is simply that performance, while by nature unlike an act of literary criticism, always has one of the same results: *it cannot avoid implying a point of view*. In other words, I think it is impossible to "do Shakespeare straight," a goal espoused very often by those who teach. This paper will be concerned, then, with the reasons why I feel this to be true, and with alternative goals, or modified ones, and with examples of

Shakespearean production that seem to me to elucidate different approaches to the problem.

One such approach is stated succinctly and usefully by Stanley Wells, a scholar and historian of the theater with much experience in observing production work: "The great Globe itself," writes Wells, "has vanished into air; so have its audiences. But the texts of the plays remain, and the effort must be made to present them in a manner that will reproduce for a modern audience the effect they may be supposed to have had upon their original audiences. It is a task in which personal opinion plays an enormous part."[1] The statement suggests—correctly—that much surrounding the original productions of Shakespeare's plays—including, perhaps, many of Shakespeare's intentions in writing them—is lost; and it suggests as well—probably as correctly—that at one time (the span of years of the plays' early performances) these intentions could be known and that the first audiences of the plays did in fact perceive them. It is Wells's opinion that the responsibility of our directors and actors is to try to discover those intentions—the way toward this goal being the texts of the plays—and then to articulate them to a contemporary audience so as to produce an effect comparable to that made upon their first audiences.

Our problem, however, is in knowing how to deal with

[1] Stanley Wells, "Shakespeare's Text on the Modern Stage," *Deutsche Shakespeare-Gesellschaft West Jahrbuch* (1967), p. 180. My debt to Dr. Wells's thoughts on Shakespearean production is greater than can be acknowledged in a single note. While this paper takes a different point of view than does his article, he has provided for me a basic approach to this subject matter for which I am most grateful.

those effects, and to admit candidly that sometimes the right effect—or *a* right one—has varying relevance to Shakespeare's intention, if we can discover it; that at times a conceptual emphasis
which in the days of the Globe and Blackfriars may have been
mirrored with parallel *effectiveness* in stage terms can be rendered no longer in this way—either because the original intention
is now obscure or because, even if we can detect it, it no longer
affects the emotions as it may have done once. In any case, intellectual understanding does not always contribute to a rich theatrical moment. There can be no question that Shakespeare's
audiences grasped—really *heard*—more of the plays than we do,
because as art objects they were conceived within patterns of
perception and response that Shakespeare and his audiences had
in common, and which were of course in many ways quite different from ours. But once we have granted that discovering Shakespeare's intentions can sometimes inform the way we produce his
plays, and even if we grant that his original audiences inferred
those intentions more ready than we do, I am not at all sure that
it is those intentions that modern actors and directors ought to
seek out and try to render in stage terms, but, in Wells's phrase,
"the effect they may be supposed to have had." Sometimes these
effects—the special theatrical impact of a moment of stage action
—are easily within an imaginative circuit between the Elizabethans and us, and when they are we have the rare opportunity to
observe something of Shakespeare's stage methods, a subject
much more difficult to discuss than his thematic concerns.

Let us examine one such moment in *Richard II.* I choose it
because it is such a useful one in teaching the play and because,
considered textually, it is also a dynamic example of clearly ar-

ticulated "thematic" concern. It is that sort of moment in the
theater when the playwright's intention is contained very clearly
within a stage effect, the stage effect itself implicit in the text.
Richard stands facing the usurper Bolingbroke, holding the most
important stage property of the Elizabethan theater.

> Here, cousin, seize the crown. Here, cousin,
> On this side my hand, and on that side yours.
> Now is this golden crown like a deep well
> That owes two buckets, filling one another,
> The emptier ever dancing in the air,
> The other down, unseen, and full of water.
> That bucket down and full of tears am I,
> Drinking my griefs,

(and here Richard would probably have removed his hand)

> whilst you mount up on high.
> (IV.i.181–88)

Obviously this moment represented for the Elizabethans, as to an
extent it can for us, a living emblem of abdication and usurpation of the English crown; Richard himself sees to it that the act
is dramatized and not simply described. The moment provides
an easy approach to Tudor conceptions of kingship behind all
of Shakespeare's histories, as well as many of his other plays, and
of course such theory in this instance vividly informs the staging.
But the scene is not "about" that theory, and a modern director
anxious to find the effectiveness of the text for a modern audience would do better to turn to the character of his hero rather
than to the emblematic prop in his hands. In this lucky instance
when Shakespeare's theatrical emphasis is charged with psycho-

logical material as accessible to us as it was to the Elizabethans, our director will discover, hopefully, that *Richard II* as a play is much more concerned with the way in which its hero gives up his crown than with the way Henry Bolingbroke usurps it. The great danger in assuming that one can act or direct Shakespeare "straight" is not only in the mistaken notion that we can always perceive as his original audiences may have perceived, but in the erroneous idea that if we could do so we should find the clues to production in a philosophical energy and not in a theatrical— and hence a human and personal—one. Shakespeare's *Richard II* is about a king who gives up his crown in a fascinating, self-dramatizing, often perverse way, and then, in some terms, finds his manhood. Tudor views of kingship inform the action of this play, but the play is not about them. Similarly, an awareness of Renaissance Christianity's understanding of the sin of despair, an awareness of the theological description of the inevitable damnation that follows it, and an awareness of the Elizabethans' feelings about necromancy and of the misuses of nature and intellect —all explain much that is absolutely basic to *Dr. Faustus*; but Marlowe's play is no more "about" these matters than *Richard II* is "about" the responsibilities of kingship and the dangers of usurpation, or *Lear* "about" the great hierarchies of society and nature—no matter how vitally such materials of intellectual history may relate to these texts. Richard's crown is not so important a symbol for modern audiences, American or English, as it must have been for Shakespeare's; and modern audiences know both less and more about science—and perhaps about black magic!—than did Marlowe's. But this does not mean that the behavior of King Richard and Faustus can never be theatrically vivid for us, although the degree to which we feel their motivations and responses explicable in terms of our own is relative. Faustus' great cry, "See, see, where Christ's blood streams in the firmament!/ One drop would save my soul, half a drop . . ." refers to a belief to which we may or may not respond "feelingly," but what is certain is that we can grasp his anguish as deeply as any Elizabethan could.

It is in reproducing the effect of such moments that modern productions find their greatest challenge, and only rarely do an actor's lines, a stage property, and an explicit intention on the part of the playwright meet so conveniently as they do in the abdication scene of *Richard II*. Some modern productions, however, have found correlatives of theatrical impact within many of the plays, and these suggest an approach to those vast stretches of the texts where total recall, so to speak, is impossible. The life of a play may be articulated in a manner that varies considerably from what we know of original production conditions and methods, yet remain nevertheless in the largest sense "Shakespearean." Such methods of production are very hard to describe, but I will try to give some examples of them. Obviously, it is the degree to which any modern production varies from what we know, or think we know, of Elizabethan methods that provides most ground for debate—perhaps especially among members of the academic profession who attend Shakespearean productions with some frequency.[2] Some directors—mainly those attracted to stud-

[2] Peter Brook's description of scholars at the theater should make most of us wince, but the shoe fits too perfectly not to quote him, and, as he has borne in the past few years perhaps more often than he has deserved the attacks of scholars (particularly in this coun-

ies of stage history—prefer to stage Shakespeare under conditions as close as possible (in their view) to the Elizabethan way; others, in Wells's words, "believe that the plays can make their true effect only when they are rewritten, recostumed, recomposed, restaged, reset, and generally reconstituted. . . . There is moreover a third class . . . made up of those whose prime concern in staging a play of Shakespeare's is not to put across the body or the idea of the original . . . but rather to construct a theatrical event which will work in its independent way."[3] These are very categorical descriptions of the preferences of our directors (and audiences), and I have overgeneralized Wells's presentation of them; but the categories may be useful for our own discussion.

---

try), to quote him at length. He is speaking of a sort of theater he finds "Deadly," as containing no potential either for growth or immediate theatrical excitement: "The Deadly Theater takes easily to Shakespeare. We see his plays done by good actors in what seems to be the proper way—they look lively and colorful, there is music and everyone is all dressed up, just as they are supposed to be in the best of classical theaters. Yet secretly we find it excruciatingly boring—and in our hearts we either blame Shakespeare, or theater as such, or even ourselves. To make matters worse there is always a deadly spectator, who for special reasons enjoys a lack of intensity and even a lack of entertainment, such as the scholar who emerges from routine performances of the classics smiling because nothing has distracted him from trying over and confirming his pet theories to himself, whilst reciting his favorite lines under his breath. In his heart he sincerely wants a theater that is nobler-than-life and he confuses a sort of intellectual satisfaction with the true experience for which he craves. Unfortunately, he lends the weight of his authority to dullness and so the Deadly Theater goes on its way" (*The Empty Space* [New York, 1968], p. 10).

[3] Wells, *Deutsche Shakespeare-Gesellschaft West Jahrbuch*, p. 181.

I suggest that the first way—to attempt a staging as close as possible to the Elizabethan procedure, so far as we know it—is essentially untheatrical and pointless. Even though the physical nature of Shakespeare's theaters and the styles of his actors are to some extent discoverable, to rerender them would result only in a rather dull form of archeology—and never in vivid theatrical action. As Professor E. H. Gombrich has observed in his great study of the graphic arts and human understanding of them,[4] successful art reminds us of reality simply because art mirrors not nature but the artist's perceptions of nature. When we recognize common ground between an artist's way of seeing reality and our own, we can see nature—or human nature—in his work. Sometimes his way of seeing is typical enough of his time that we come to recognize it as a part of a nameable style, and we call it a convention. The history of style is therefore the history of human perception itself. The phenomenon of drama is exhilarating because it is intensely pleasurable to see people on a stage who seem to be *real*—and this apparent reality can encompass a wide range of styles of production. If what is happening onstage does not seem to be realistic human behavior, if we are unable to feel, even if we cannot say, *why* a character does or says a certain thing, then something essentially undramatic is taking place. A production set in the Elizabethan mode—accurately, if that were possible, or approximately, to the limits of our ability— would set forth human behavior realistic only to Elizabethans, except in those rare instances when their "vocabulary of motif"

---

[4] E. H. Gombrich, *Art and Illusion* (Bollingen Series XXXV.5, A. W. Mellon Lectures in the Fine Arts, 1956) (New York, 1960). See especially pp. 63–66, 85, 90, 131, 175, 356.

(in Gombrich's phrase) has not been lost in the flux of time, and we recognize it. Shakespeare was performed "straight" only during Shakespeare's lifetime, and not for very long after it, and teachers and scholars should not complain if a production of Shakespeare attempts to be "modern" in some way—what else can it aim to be, if we are to find understandable human behavior in it? A commitment to the achievements of the past and its relevance to the present must never be allowed to obscure the fact that it cannot be relived. Members of the academy are perhaps particularly protective of the past, but its literal resuscitation in drama can never be more than an empty gesture. It can never be directly relevant, never deeply involving, never truly exciting— and most important and, for historical scholars, perhaps, most ironic—it can never really achieve the noble purpose of understanding Shakespeare's intentions. If Shakespeare is to continue to be as theatrically valid as most of us tend to claim he is without giving much thought to a matter that seems so obvious, then we must be alert to those phenomena of the theater that really *do* involve and exhilarate us, which help us perceive performance of the great texts realistically. We should never forget that the revolutionary productions by Poel and Granville-Barker in the first third of this century would seem now very dated to us, and in any case hardly accurate renderings either of the texts or of the staging of Shakespeare's time; they were as typical in their way of their years as Garrick's Shakespeare was of his, or Kean's, Macready's, Tree's, or, for that matter, Gielgud's, were of theirs.

I prefer a kind of "reconstituted" Shakespeare, to use Wells's adjective, but with the qualification that such productions be based, so far as it is possible, on those clues within the texts that help us grasp the *theatrical effects* of the originals—and it is in recognizing these when they appear that historical scholarship is most helpful. It is delightful and reassuring, by the way, to observe how many great actors and directors at times come intuitively in the course of their work to decisions and choices that corroborate, or are corroborated by, some conclusions of criticism and scholarship, reached after detailed research and years of thought and reconsideration. For me, two examples of Shakespeare so reconstituted were the performances of Sir Laurence Olivier as Othello (in 1964) and of Paul Scofield as Macbeth (in 1967). Although I cannot describe each performance in detail, let me try to indicate why each of them seemed to me to answer the theatrical requirements of modern productions of Shakespeare.

In a way, actors of Othello and Macbeth are challenged by a similar problem—a problem relating, as it happens, to a point about both of these characters made clear for us by a historical and scholarly understanding of the Elizabethans' view of evil and its potential strength. Both plays are made richer when we remember that they contain much more than those rubrics suggest by which they were described—at least to me—in secondary school: as a tragedy "of jealousy" and a tragedy "of ambition." Jealous Othello surely is, and Macbeth is ambitious—but the modern actor must ask, interestingly enough, the same questions asked by the inquisitive student: where do the jealousy and the ambition come from, and why are they so overwhelmingly *personal*, so clearly typical in scope of everything else in the lives of these two men? The Elizabethans' awareness that neither Iago nor the witches could have succeeded had not Othello and Macbeth somehow been prepared for their visitations greatly helps the modern actor and his director who may have come by intuition or research to the same conclusion—a conclusion perfectly suited to current acting techniques and role preparation: that the horror is first conceived *inside* Othello and Macbeth, and not outside them, and that just as Mephistophilis could not succeed had Faustus not called him in the first place, so the sexual ego and possessiveness that eventually prepare Othello to succumb to Iago and "the swelling act/ Of the imperial theme" that already corrupts Macbeth's imagination are rooted deeply in the consciousness—or subconsciousness—of each hero before the evil appears on stage in external shape. One could say simply that they are men psychologically ready for what is to happen, and this readiness was manifest in the performances of Olivier as Othello and Scofield as Macbeth, thus making the behavior of the characters perceivable, acceptable, human.

The work of both actors in preparing their roles was extensive and detailed; from the results of this work, one can choose only a few. There was Olivier's brilliant physical presentation of Othello, amazingly convincing for a man who stands actually only a bit over five feet ten inches—onstage, in this production, because of his charismatic presence, apparently well over six feet; the sensuous roll of his gait, the easy turns, the carriage of a man obviously in battle trim yet whose energies could be totally luxurious and specifically sexual, suggesting a dangerous narcissism; the vocal preparation that allowed an extra octave of bass range when it was wanted; the careful choice and use of properties— the long-stemmed, blood-red rose, for example, with which he played, lightly, absent-mindedly, in his first scene, or the heavy cross suspended from his neck, reminding us—and him?—that Othello has been a Christian warrior in the employ of a Christian state, yet torn loose and thrown to the winds with the force of gigantic agony, as he knelt to his old pagan and exotic gods, the marble heavens and the tides of the Pontic, the Propontic, and the Hellespont, the gesture following Iago's "Your mind may change," on his "Never, Iago!" (III.iii.449–50). Throughout the vocalizations *filled* the character: the subtle yet audible emphases given all the personal pronouns, for example, in those speeches to the senate in which Othello defines so eloquently what he is and —a consideration of immense importance to the actor—how emphatically he believes in himself; and, later in the play, the vocal placement, emphasis, and pacing given, for example, those lines in which Othello identifies himself with those so great that they are born to be betrayed, self-confidence merging with his huge self-pity through an infinitely subtle trick of the voice, a nuance of phrasing:

> Haply for I am black
> And have not those soft parts of conversation
> That chamberers have, or for I am declined
> Into the vale of years—yet that's not much—
> She's gone. I am abused, and my relief
> Must be to loathe her. O curse of marriage,
> That we can call these delicate creatures ours,
> And not their appetites! I had rather be a toad
> And live upon the vapor of a dungeon
> Than keep a corner in the thing I love
> For others' uses. Yet 'tis the plague to great ones;
> Prerogatived are they less than the base.

'Tis destiny unshunnable, like death.
Even then this forkèd plague is fated to us
When we do quicken. . . .

(III.iii.262–76)[5]

For the actor playing Macbeth, the problem is at once simpler and harder; his lines suggest, but do not make explicit, the inner readiness for corruption I tried to describe earlier. This is in any case a matter of the degree of emphasis found by the actor in rehearsal and private thought. The hero's rendering of any speech can be made to affect the audience's apprehension of his inner state in many subtle ways—specifically, the nature of the surprise or shock he feels when confronted by the witches, or, later in the play, by the vision of the dagger. Scofield's reaction was prepared brilliantly by Macbeth's very first line in the play, the delivery of which I can describe only as charged with an awareness of surrounding time and place, both in terms of the military victories just achieved and in terms of whatever the physical context of the action was conceived to be. We had seen, in more or less traditional terms (yet set forth with staggering theatrical power), the personifications of the witches, the armies of Duncan, their leather and furred clothing crusted with blood, only the King himself in clean and shining white, absolutely saint-like, "clear in his great office," the bleeding Captain, one

[5] Happily, Sir Laurence's performance has been preserved on phonograph records; the recording (RCA Victor album VDS-100) was taped at a special performance, and not in a studio-reading, and is therefore a much more accurate archive of the production. The phrasing and specific nuances to which I refer may be heard throughout, of course, but perhaps best in the speeches on Sides 1, 4, and 5 (containing I.iii and III.iii).

horrid scar of battle, collapsing finally to the earth—earth made
of a huge shaggy ruglike material that covered the whole stage,
capable of assuming in different lights the texture of a realistic
heath or an open wound, ranging in color from a deep rust to
crimson to black; then the witches again, then the drum, and then
—a stroke of genius, I think, on the part of the director, Peter
Hall—Macbeth's entrance alone, not with Banquo, who came on
after the hero's first line. Here Scofield walked, a tall man to
begin with, huge against the smoky red of the stage, his battle
sword across the shoulder, held with the easy grace of a soldier
familiar with his weapon, his eyes cast up and out, beyond his
own path, all the way from upstage center to the very lip of the
narrow protruding apron, all in that utter silence of anticipation
and attention that can be commanded by the simple presence of
a great actor, and, finally, conveying somehow the sense of a man
who knows and feels too much that hasn't yet a name, in his deep
Sussex twang, pacing the sounds and silences of the line with the
intuitive understanding that came from long rehearsals full of
trial and error, "So foul and fair a day I have not seen." Then on
came Banquo, businesslike with his question about the distance
to Forres, then seeing suddenly those crouching shapes in the
shadows; but even as Banquo exclaimed, we paid less attention to
him than to Macbeth, whose gaze had now swung toward them,
his eyes clouded, no movement or gesture signifying shock, but
only a feeling that the whole man, mind and body, had assimi-
lated what he saw and felt a deep reverberation in his memory
by the time he too addressed them: "Speak, if you can: what are
you?" We have all of us felt evil within us (whatever name we
have given it), and Scofield let us understand how a great man

had felt it greatly, had not yet succumbed to it, yet had at his fingertips, so to speak, dangerously ready in his memory that "horrid image" of the witches' "suggestion." Later, of course, the great and so often clichéd soliloquy on the dagger became part of the texture of everything that had gone before in Macbeth's mind: it did indeed "[marshal him] the way that [he] was going."

I grant that these two examples of "reconstituted" Shakespeare deal with material for which modern rendering could find good correlatives in Elizabethan psychology; methods of work are different, but the stage *effect* is where Shakespeare put it: in the composition of human character productive of behavioral responses. Reconstitution, it must be stated clearly, does not always retain so much of the original in its literal form. I should like to turn to another modern production which, while deeply illuminating the text at hand, to a great extent remolded and reshaped it while retaining at base the implicit force and theatricality of Shakespeare's work—Orson Welles's film of the *Henry IV* plays called *Chimes at Midnight* (in this country, simply *Falstaff*). The fact that we are dealing with a different art form does not alter, I think, some of the principles we have been discussing.

Welles's movie is essentially a kaleidoscopic revisualization of Shakespeare's two plays. Scenes are set in new sequence, many of them cut entirely, others formed of the original text intact but with lines from elsewhere in the plays inserted for conceptual emphasis—either ironic or corroborative, some of the characters eliminated, but those remaining never destructively oversimplified. Amazingly, into two and a half hours of film time, Welles has set forth the psychological reality of these plays, taking as his dynamic center the same core of deep human emotion that energizes Shakespeare's texts—the struggle within Prince Hal simultaneously to love, to resist, and to survive two parents, one his father and the other a surrogate, and to choose from among several life styles one that is uniquely and triumphantly his. As is the case with *Richard II*, a historical understanding of Tudor views of kingship can enrich our understanding of the Shakespeare chronicles; more directly informative at times about the major characters of the *Henry IV* plays are those lumpy yet somehow attractive moral interludes of the sixteenth century. Shakespeare's drama, once again, is filled with living stage emblems of the personal and political conflicts that form their narrative content. To speak only of one such moment, Hal, after Shrewsbury, stands lonely and triumphant between the dead body of Hotspur and the apparently dead Falstaff; one thinks of many parallel moments in the old interludes when Youth—call him Lusty Juventus, even Mankind—triumphs over the temptations of Pride on the one hand and Revelry on the other, and no doubt the line of descent to that moment at the end of *1 Henry IV* is a direct one. But the history of this dramaturgy will not make the behavior of Shakespeare's characters closer to our grasp, and it is perhaps particularly true of the histories that this behavior—in terms of motive and response—most frequently eludes us, whether we attempt to teach these plays or to produce them. What Welles has achieved in *Falstaff* is to find a way to make this action absolutely realistic in psychological terms not far, if at all, removed from Shakespeare's. He has placed his emphasis where it is in Shakespeare, and so often is not in modern productions—upon the Prince himself. The King, Falstaff, and Hotspur move about him, come tangent to him, but never do we forget what these scenes are *about*.

Welles himself, of course, portrays Falstaff—and although I was almost invariably irritated by his underenergized line readings, his intention was clear, and it supported the plan of the over-all project (an amazing achievement for this great director and actor, who has not in the past so successfully suppressed his own ego!); jovial he can be, but predominantly he is sad. A man with the depth of emotion and intellect to be witty in himself while evoking wit in other men will not necessarily be—nor is he likely to be—the clean and happy, pink-cheeked master of the revels we so often find in our Falstaffs. This is a fat old man more often than not quiet and introspective, yet the embodiment of personal license, shown to be dying of drink and, in all probability, tertiary syphillis, who does not tempt the Prince because he is descended from the Vice, nor boast because he is related to the *Miles gloriosus*, but does both because he is desperately attracted to, loves, and requires Prince Hal's youth and promise, and because he knows that Hal—far from being only superficially amused with him—loves him and understands him, even if that understanding clearly carries with it an element of contempt. King Henry IV is played by Sir John Gielgud, a brilliant casting decision. He too is dying, and although the Jerusalem Chamber is not made much of in the film, the process of death is supported by constant references to the King's guilt—shown to be as much a cause of death as old age. He feels little if any warmth for his son, but his political consciousness is razor-sharp, and the actor's major intention is to show the politician's consuming desire for an heir equal to his understanding of kingship. Henry Monmouth, between these two old and dying men, is only beginning to live, and must choose not only between them but between two views of the world, both of which, with Hotspur's, he is to reject.

It was easier for Shakespeare to write Prince Hal into the center of his plays than it is for any modern actor or director to keep him there; not only do Falstaff or Hotspur threaten to swamp him, but his own stage life exists often in terms of stage conventions we no longer perceive as conveying reality. The most important, and the most difficult, of these is that component of stage narrative in Elizabethan plays in which a character seems (to us) to step outside the action, comment upon it, even anticipate it, such as Hal does at the end of the second scene of *1 Henry IV*. Not only the device itself, but the subject matter of Hal's soliloquy, is difficult. Even if we discount as uninformed or as insensitive those readers who would infer the Prince priggish or Machiavellian or both, as he anticipates his own kingship, his useful playing holidays, and the way he will appear to men when he banishes his tavern companions, the speech remains a remarkably hard one for any modern actor. In Shakespeare's stage terms, it was essentially theatrical and engaging; in ours, it is potentially untheatrical and even dull. To whom is it addressed? Although it is partially apostrophic, how are those sections and phrases that are purely introspective to be rendered so as to be felt by a modern audience as expressions of a warm and generous young man? Welles's answer not only suits the requirement of the modern director—who would demand of the text a reason for the Prince to speak the lines in the first place—but is actually a more "Shakespearean" solution than I have seen in most productions following the apparently straighter and narrower line. He moves the speech from its place in the text to one where it is much clearer, for both Hal and the audience watching him, that Falstaff has offended and irritated him; the talk of the robbery, which precedes the speech in the text, is in the film augmented by a full tavern scene that allows the Prince to set his personal objective against exactly that social context of revelry that opposes it— just as Falstaff opposes any king who would hang thieves. Although the speech is a soliloquy in the text, Welles does not leave Hal alone, but makes the camera track Falstaff, following Hal as he leaves the tavern door, watching him eagerly for any sign of anger or affection, the old man almost constantly in the background of the frame, slightly out of focus, while close up we see the Prince's face as he speaks softly aloud—in very realistic reaction to his situation—his feelings about his companions, his role, and his future. Keith Baxter, who played Hal for Welles, speaks the speech with great honesty, as well as with a good sense of the verse, and powerfully projects the irony in his perception that one day he will in fact "pay the debt [he] never promisèd" —not only to become King of England and to cleanse the land, but to succeed his father, to become his own man. Such moments as these give richness to the life of such a son, who must remind us of any son who realizes in pain and grief that, actually or metaphorically, he must replace his father. If today all roads lead to Vienna as in Shakespeare's day they led to Jerusalem, it remains true that a psychological depth of character here can reconstitute with validity the shape of Shakespeare's text. Just as the man, Richard II, is at the center of his play, and the crown itself a meaningful object only because of human uses of it, so in his direction of Baxter as Prince Henry Welles reminds us that the agony of father and son informs the *Henry IV* plays, and, indeed, makes much more meaningful the political significance that stands beyond the paternal theme.

Throughout the film, quick, almost frenetic, alternation of camera shots emphasizes alternation between youth and age in the characters.[6] The repeated image-motif of Shallow and Falstaff as they move painfully through heavy snow silently falling upon the English countryside is a beautiful emblem of the end of life, of the exhausted, dying elements in the nation. The social consciousness of the movie is as alert as Shakespeare's, and thematically pertinent in Shakespearean terms too: vast, forbidding castle walls dominate the dirty stucco of the tavern, and the footage of the Battle of Shrewsbury itself must be some of the finest, truest, ugliest scenes of warfare ever shot and edited for a movie. Throughout, small directorial touches make direct and accessible the thematic center Welles has chosen for his reconstitution of the plays. As the King angrily dismisses Northumberland from council, for example, he emphasizes with both pace and stress the one word that reminds us of the conflict and jealousy in his mind as he compares his own Henry with that other one: "My lord Northumberland, we license your departure with your . . . *son*" (my punctuation and italics); later, Bolingbroke's breath freezes with every word into small puffs of vapor as he berates his own son in the cold sunlight of the castle hall, and, with the petulance of the old and self-pitying, he ignores Hal's oath to defeat Hotspur in battle. This is an omission that emphasizes,

[6] I am indebted to one of my former students at Harvard, Mr. Peter Jaszi, for his perceptive comments about Welles's film.

perhaps overpurifies, an ironic rivalry of viewpoint—just as, during the battle scenes, Welles omits Hal's rescue of his father from Douglas. Shakespeare's method is richer and more varied in texture, here and elsewhere, but the omissions, for example, do not make the King seem a less detailed personality in the movie than he does in the plays—simply because, I think, the movie finds the dynamic impulse for action under the text. Welles's film is a *reimaging* of the texts. In cutting the text, much is lost, but the director's rearrangement is not irresponsible, for it emphasizes an underlying statement in Shakespeare's text itself: the *effect*, theatrically, may be supposed to be close to the one intended. One might almost speak, in fact, of Welles's dramatization of the plays' *sub*text. "Subtext" is a term often misused in post-Stanislavsky acting schools, but it has a very useful meaning for the study of any drama, even drama in which the verbal element is as powerful as it is in Shakespeare. Stanislavsky meant by "subtext" simply that line of intention, of motivation, that might exist beneath the actual words of a script. The implications of subtextual investigation in rehearsals are perhaps more obvious for plays in the modern repertory than for those of Shakespeare. Characters in contemporary drama, for one reason or another, do not at times say what they really mean—most often because the playwright wants our ironic awareness to become part of his total effect. Shakespeare's characters, as Stoll observed long ago, almost always say what they mean—or, one might say, what they want to mean—unless they are consciously lying, and when this happens we know it, too. Nevertheless, the technique of finding a character's intention in a Shakespearean speech or scene—the technique of discussing, at least, the possibility of a subtextual element—can serve a valuable purpose in modern productions, provided the technique is carried forward with common sense. It can be most useful to the modern director or actor when there exists in the text a conventional gesture—a speech, an action, the use of a property—that we sense, or which research tells us, would have been immediately understood by an Elizabethan audience, but the significance of which is lost for us. At times such as these it may well serve a genuine purpose to try to ask ourselves what it is, quite simply, the character wants to do, to what he may be reacting, what he hopes may happen. When these questions are asked, we may discover—as in Welles's direction of Prince Hal's soliloquy—that human psychology provides a behavioral answer that is not so distant from the Shakespearean intention, so far as we can know it.

This leads directly to that third class of current productions described by Stanley Wells—those that are directed so as to become "theatrical [events] which will work in [their] independent way"; or which, one might add, are so thoroughly "reconstituted" as to appear a different play, a new work for the stage. One should make a firm distinction between these, by the way, and a simple "jollying-up" of a text, as in some of the brilliantly wrongheaded, happily irresponsible productions of Tyrone Guthrie. The best example of this form of reimaged Shakespeare in recent years is probably Peter Brook's production of *King Lear*, with, as it happens, Paul Scofield again in the title role. Fortunately, this production was seen by so many either in this country or in England, and has been so thoroughly described in various reviews and articles, has been attacked or defended in such detail, that I need do no more, I think, than summarize what I take to be its intention and its special effectiveness.

The production was conceived in terms of a universe much as Samuel Beckett might describe it—or at least as Beckett might as interpreted by Jan Kott, whose essay about the play strongly influenced Brook's direction and rehearsal procedures. It depicted, in short, a dead or dying universe, in which the evil or blindness of individual men and women, or their frustrated attempts to communicate with each other, inevitably cause their extinction in a mood more of catatonic grief and dullness than of protest or verbalized agony. Setting, costumes, and vocal levels all emphasized this mood and tone. Yet no production in modern theater proves so clearly, I think, that cutting alone is not the most important factor in altered staging of Shakespeare today: the promptbook for this production, filed in the Shakespeare Center at Stratford-upon-Avon, accessible for easy comparison with the promptbooks for all other Royal Shakespeare Company productions, reveals that Brook's cuts were fewer and much more conservative than those for many other stagings of *Lear*—productions we might willingly call Shakespeare served up "straight." His most important cuts were Folio cuts in any case. It is what happened onstage that made the production, however brilliant, essentially un-Shakespearean. After Gloucester's blinding, he was painfully tormented by Cornwall's servants, and the kindness shown toward him by one of them was eliminated; Goneril and Regan were given loud and extended cause for their complaints against the knights in Lear's train, and the evil intentions of these daughters were mitigated, an important distortion of the text; the repentance of Edmund at the end of the play was cut, and, as the great deaths in the last scene occurred, they were made unimportant in this production by others' monotonic observation of them. Finally, Edgar lugged the guts of his dead brother off into the dusty haze upstage, the other characters left on unmoved and unmoving—the dead and the near-dead only so many rocks in a dead landscape, all of them bearing only the most distant resemblance to human beings. The effect of all this was, for me, very powerful; but it had nothing to do with Shakespeare, who intended to show—no matter how difficult it may be many times to know his purpose—that men are at least not blind to the inner resources of love, that suffering can dignify even if ultimately it obliterates, that the tolerance of the world is oriented more favorably toward good men than toward evil men, and that if good men die, their importance, if they can achieve the insight implicit in a tragic action, is rather clear to the society in which they have lived, and is not obscured from it.

But let me suggest that to argue these points is in some sense a waste of time. Brook's irresponsibility, if one can call it that, is that of an important creative artist engaged in a part of his craft, and I do not think he should be attacked; his major offense, if offense it be, was to compose a paraphrase in a new mode on an old text and not to call our attention to the fact that he had done so. Beyond this, it is important to see what Brook and others like him have done rather than to slap their wrists petulantly. The act of theater is not like an act of scholarship, nor is the performance of a play remotely like editing one, for living drama must view a text as a starting point for further creativity. The major problem in works of criticism such as those by Kott and works for the theater such as those by Brook is that, unlike the works of Shakespeare, they are philosophical. Shakespeare's world, however one may wish to describe it, or whichever part of it is chosen for detailed analysis, is ultimately imponderable and may not be reduced to an abstract statement, whereas the work of such directors as Peter Brook often seeks to make a statement *about* the world—Shakespeare's and our own. As it happens, the world of Beckett does not really illuminate Shakespeare's, but it does help to make a statement about ours. In some way, Brook has written an essay about *Lear* much as Brecht wrote one about *Coriolanus,* and he has done so by altering, by reconstituting, the very molecular structure of the original, by paraphrasing the text in a new medium of theater.

Remember that we do not condemn as irresponsible Boito and Verdi on *Othello,* Liszt on *Don Giovanni,* Picasso on the portraits of Rembrandt, or Busoni or Schoenberg on Bach. We recognize some paraphrases as new and different works, and to argue that their vaguely parallel movement is not "accurate" is a waste of critical energy. They may be in themselves bad works or good works; they may teach us something new about the original; most likely, they will tell us something about the age in which they were conceived. Brook on the text of Shakespeare is, I think, an analogous phenomenon. An achievement of scholarship in this century has been to affirm the "integrity" of Shakespeare's text: the modes of the language, the sequence of scenes, the over-all structures of the plays. All has been investigated, it seems, and we know, or think we know, that very little in a play by Shakespeare is there by accident. It is true, of course, that any director who chooses to disturb this texture of action usually does so to his own peril. But that does not mean that he *must* not alter it. The director's job is a relatively new one in theater history; it is not likely, for example, that anything like his function as we know it existed in Shakespeare's theater. In these years he has become an increasingly powerful figure, and is currently more important than any leading actor in most productions. Mainly because of such a phenomenon as Brook's productions represent, a director is thought to be responsible for a conceptual statement as well as a theatrical one. I do not think this is necessarily a dangerous development; any strong and cumulative effect onstage must be the result of one man's vision of Shakespeare's art. But its virtues or shortcomings depend on the man at work, and must be described in terms of individual productions. Brook himself has produced some very "straight" and very pallid Shakespeare. Nominally, the director of the Olivier *Othello* was John Dexter, but I doubt very much that he had more to say about Olivier's readings than Olivier himself, or, perhaps, than Mr. Kenneth Tynan.

A director must work today with the living personalities of his actors. He really has no other option, except to refuse to acknowledge the events of his own times. A sense of ensemble onstage—that most highly regarded achievement among the great repertory companies of the past—remains an achievement possible only in terms of work with human behavior and not with critical theory. This method of work has parallel results in production style. If Orson Welles almost outrageously altered the texts of *1, 2 Henry IV*, there is still no denying that in this instance (the same cannot be said, I think, for his other film versions of Shakespeare) he clarified a pattern of character and behavior that rings true to the energy that informs the original texts. To remain aware of new ways to perceive reality in human action: that must be the goal of any responsible director of Shakespeare today. To do this is to evoke, surely, a richer sense of history than to attempt (what is in any case impossible) a derivative reproduction of the old style. This can only result in mannerism. One thinks of those very pretty productions of Shakespeare in the prewar years, resumed, happily only for a short time, in the late forties, usually designed by Motley and featuring some astounding elocution, but very little that we could recognize *now* as absorbing action. I grant this a drastic attitude. It involves the opinion that in other areas of drama, and in other art forms, too, some works no longer pertain to our lives in any important way. For my money, Shaw's Caesar's views on war, love, and honorable empire as almost as empty as Respighi's on Roman festivals. One must be grateful for the energy of the practicing artist, for although he may seem to call attention only to himself—and, indeed, may have intended nothing more than that!—he actually turns our attention to the work itself, to the processes of creativity in Shakespeare. The mysteries of those processes invite experimentation and innovation. If they did not, they would no longer be mysteries and we should have discovered long ago their dull and lifeless answers.

Robert Hapgood

SHAKESPEARE AND THE INCLUDED SPECTATOR

THE POLYVISION EXHIBITION, CZECHOSLOVAKIAN PAVILION, EXPO 67, MONTREAL

LIKE A MODEL, Polyvision embodies the texture of a Shakespearean play. With its multiple projectors and moving geometrical shapes, it makes mechanical and visual the constant interrelation of perspectives that is the natural idiom of Shakespeare's dialogue and action. On cubes sliding back and forth it shows a car at an early stage of assembly; at the same time, on a whirling cylinder and other forms, are other cars at later stages; while on a wide screen at the rear is a freeway scene. Then it moves quickly on to further industrial themes. The effect is of a thirty-three-ring circus. Myriad-minded was Coleridge's word for it in Shakespeare.

Most Shakespearean of all (Shakespeare was central in the development of Czech theater) is the long mirror in the middle, reflecting the passing spectators. In an era of Happenings and Environments, the visible, included spectator may seem the latest

The playgoing on which this essay is based was supported in part by a grant from the Central University Research Fund of the University of New Hampshire.

experimental thing, but he was of course thoroughly at home in the Elizabethan theater. Where I can put myself in the polyvisual picture, Shakespeare's spectator might sit onstage.

Shakespeare's commentators rarely look at themselves as spectators in his mirror or consider his text from the audience's point of view—as a scenario for a spectator experience. They are much more likely to ask what happens in *Hamlet* than what happens at *Hamlet*. Yet can a play come to full life without a spontaneous Happening between its performance and its spectators? Can a commentator be more sure of anything than of his own responses?

THE OREGON SHAKESPEAREAN FESTIVAL, ASHLAND, 1961

Five weeks of watching daily rehearsals and nightly performances makes me see that Elizabethan playgoing was fundamentally different from modern playgoing.

The most suggestive and authentic feature of Ashland's Elizabethan-style productions is that there are no intermissions. The result is a radical change in my customary economy of attention. Instead of building with the actors to a strong curtain, I sit back, as at a movie, and let the scenes roll by. Yet, again as at a movie, I am never totally released from the hold of the performance. Instead, with its fuller texts, Ashland provides the relaxations that Shakespeare himself built in. So in the 1961 *Hamlet* the humorous scene between Polonius and Reynaldo, usually cut, makes a reassuring return to this world after the otherworldly episodes just past, while carrying on the theme of the pompously insistent father and lightly suggesting the habitual suspicion of Claudius' court.

Continuous action thus helps to make the dramatic event a single experience. It was one of many sources of unity in the Elizabethan theater—with its unchanging façade, its constant daylight, its all-male cast, its steadily throbbing pentameters. With so secure a center, Elizabethan playwrights could afford to take liberties with the unities of theme and tone to which modern performers and critics hold so humorlessly. Will these unities someday seem as mechanical as the unities of time and place seem today?

Freedom and relaxation must have characterized the Elizabethan theatrical situation generally. At a conventional modern performance I expect to be "enthralled." I am boxed and hushed in the dark auditorium, my attention held by detailed sets, pinpointed by elaborate lighting, and intensified to "gripping" climaxes. Shakespeare at Ashland drives with much looser reins. At most he commands (not demands) my attention at critical moments. Otherwise I can relax in the supple amplitude of his style, sure that no necessary question of the play will escape me, yet rewarded to the full extent of my attention. (Contrast the anxious modern director who cuts his texts so extensively that one must strain for each word.) If a modern spectator is treated like a willing slave, Shakespeare's spectator is treated like a king.

Henry IV, PHOENIX THEATER, ON TELEVISION

Modern directors seem intent on reducing Shakespeare to a one-ring circus, presumably for spectators too simple-minded to follow more. How is the first line of this play to be read? "So shaken as we are, so wan with care . . ." As in every other version I have seen, the Phoenix King Henry delivers it straight. He is simply shaken and wan. Yet clearly this is a pseudo-event: the king already knows that the wish to lead an expiatory crusade he is piously acting out is not feasible. He has already sent for Hotspur to answer for it. The Phoenix director covers his tracks by changing the key line from "I have sent for him to answer this" to "I will send for him to answer this." But he has bought clarity and simplicity at the price of subtlety and complexity. And of truth. For this version asks the spectator to take as spontaneous what Shakespeare meant to seem calculated.

Henry V, DIRECTED BY RONALD WATKINS, HARROW, ENGLAND, 1962

Where Ashland performances are done at night with modern lighting, performances at Harrow begin in the sunlight of early evening and end with ordinary electric lights. Again the simulation of Elizabethan conditions liberates the spectator. Instead of spotlighting the principals, the scope of my attention is widened —to include, for example, the Boy in *Henry V*, and the often silent perspective which, in his self-possessed fashion, he casts on the ways of his elders. Again, also, the effect is inclusively unifying. I cannot avoid seeing the other spectators—they are in the foreground and, on the other side of the thrust stage, in the background. We are all as visibly there as the actors. We share the same light with the actors, who can see us.

Richard III, OLD GLOBE PLAYHOUSE, SAN DIEGO, CALIFORNIA, 1961

I listen to Queen Margaret delivering her curse, but it is Douglas Watson as Richard III that I watch, as (like me) he watches and listens. Even when he is silent, Richard dominates the stage. That is a major part of his strange appeal: he is often himself a spectator, and full of brilliant foyer talk, about himself as well as others. Instead of trying to black out the reality of his spectator's observing presence, Shakespeare thus plays upon it—just as he does upon his own role as playwright (Richard is a plotter of plots) and that of his actor (he is a player of parts). Iago makes the same appeals. But Hamlet is Shakespeare's most profoundly dramatized spectator, for he shares our spectatorly inability to act and speak effectively. In turn we share his bewilderment before the enigma of these paralyses. To an alarming extent, he and we occupy the same theater. When he refers to "that fellow in the cellarage," we are as dizzy as he is at this point. Where is he?—in Elsinore? or on the stage with its "cellarage" beneath? Where are we?

Julius Caesar, THE AMERICAN SHAKESPEARE FESTIVAL, STRATFORD, CONNECTICUT, 1966

What if the houselights had been up throughout this performance? Many of the speeches were delivered toward the audience in a frankly declamatory way. If I had shared the same light with the actors, I too might have become a Roman. Then I would not

have smiled detachedly at Antony's techniques of crowd manip-
ulation. I would have been, for the moment, myself part of his
audience and swayed by him.

As a Shakespearean spectator I often have experiences analogous to those of the characters onstage. So in civil-war plays
like this one and *Richard II* I feel divided loyalties; "like to a
little kingdom" I suffer with Brutus "the nature of an insurrec-
tion." Like the characters, I must make choices on insufficient
evidence, choices which like many of them I come to regret.
Like them I am left in a quandary at the end, with no real prospect of improvement.

Macbeth, NEW YORK SHAKESPEARE FESTIVAL MOBILE
THEATER, A PLAYGROUND NEAR MORNINGSIDE PARK,
1966

Fear was the overwhelming effect of this performance. The fear-
inspiring scenes were done best—simply, directly, expertly. The
small platform suddenly swarmed with ghostly kings; Banquo
was murdered in a corner of the stage, as swiftly as in an alley.
Compounded by the private fears of a white man in a predominantly black audience, my fears as a spectator were almost as
great as those of Macbeth himself.

The street became part of the theater. The play began in
daylight, and as Macbeth's world darkened so did mine. What
better accompaniment to Macbeth's crimes than real sirens in the
intersection nearby? Their cascade during Lady Macbeth's sleep-
walk would have been too pat if planned, as would the cries of a
baby in the audience while Macduff learned of the murder of his

pretty ones. As it was, however, these aleatory effects were part of an Environment in which the play world and the real world merged.

Julius Caesar, THE M-G-M MOTION PICTURE, 1953

In every way the spectator is more vulnerable than the reader. Safe in his study the reader looks at words on a page; in the theater the spectator is exposed not only to spoken words but to the visual, aural, and kinesthetic appeals of "total theater"—all of which Shakespeare uses. Part of the impact of this film comes from the virtuoso variations its director Joseph Mankiewicz plays upon Shakespeare's nonverbal themes. Take the pattern of rise and fall. Shakespeare himself provides literal counterparts to the metaphorical ups and downs of power in Rome, as when Caesar's former underlings stand over his fallen body. But Mankiewicz makes these still more graphic by setting almost all of his picture either on steep steps or on a mountain. One instance among many is when Cassius suits action to word at "we have the falling sickness," descending the stairs from above Brutus and Casca to below them. The sense of rise and fall extends to many aspects of the production. Caesar's body is not raised at the end of Antony's oration (as it is in Shakespeare), yet the effect of Caesar's rise is achieved by the elevation of Marlon Brando's voice at the last syllable of "ruffle up your spirits" and on all of "when comes such another." The most successful effect is the downward camera-angle when Cassius beneath a towering statue of Caesar speaks of him as a colossus and of himself as an underling. At that moment I see Cassius as he sees himself.

King Lear, ACTOR'S WORKSHOP, SAN FRANCISCO, 1961

The very form of a Shakespeare play projects its central experience. *King Lear* is itself rash and brooding, exploding into storms of violence and then dwelling at length on its consequences. Torn apart by its own extreme conflicts, it goes mad (iii.ii–iv), yet manages to feel its way to the hard-won affirmations of Act iv. When these are swept away by the death of Cordelia, the play gives itself over to howls and dubious dreams. This is the experience that I as its spectator can expect to live through, more completely than any character onstage.

The trouble with this production is not that it goes mad—why shouldn't the production do what the script does?—but that it locks itself and me inside the moment of madness alone, "disorder amazed at its own coherence," as director Herbert Blau puts it. The result diminishes even the effect of madness. For when everything is wild, nothing is wild. With everyone wearing Indian costume, naked Tom looks right at home; and Lear "fantastically dressed with wild flowers" looks no more outlandish than Lear the tribal chief.

Titus Andronicus, NEW YORK SHAKESPEARE FESTIVAL, CENTRAL PARK, 1967

If Titus must suffer enormities, so must I in watching them. At first I simply grieve with him and vicariously protest. But as one atrocity piles on another, they pass beyond the grotesque to the ludicrous. Shakespeare's most brilliant stroke in this extraordinary play is Titus' laugh when the heads of his sons are delivered.

Then if ever "the worst returns to laughter." If he had not laughed, I would have had to. As it is, Titus can then carry me with him the rest of the way from grief to fury. Not only do I want Titus to strike back at his enemies and destroy them but also I want to do so! The emotional flow from suffering to retaliation is compelling.

Yet not all-compelling. For Shakespeare does not mean for me to lose myself altogether in his play world. As always there is real basis for this: he knows as well as Dr. Johnson that a spectator never forgets that he is in a theater. Shakespeare trusts that I will respond not only with but to his play. Hence he risks the peripety of the dramatic event he seeks upon his spectators' revulsion from Titus' Ovidian banquet and killing of Lavinia. Titus has gone too far, has become the worst case of the evils he would purge, and must be purged himself. I assent to his death.

(This is a favorite Elizabethan spectator scenario. I finally pull back in the same way from such compelling overreachers as Hieronimo, Tamburlaine, Mosca.)

Shakespeare never allows us wholly to leave our responses up to his protagonists. He always places us in a position to see around their conceptions of themselves. If he invites us like Othello to idealize Desdemona, trust Iago, and make strict judgments, he also shows the fatality of these attitudes.

King Lear, THE AMERICAN SHAKESPEARE FESTIVAL, STRATFORD, CONNECTICUT, 1965

In particular, it is Shakespeare's spectators, not his heroes, who experience the fullest tragic "recognition." Such wisdom as his heroes gain through their suffering is usually incomplete and short-lived. They characteristically die into their favorite dreams —Cleopatra's marriage-in-death to Antony being the most glorious instance.

As played by Morris Carnovsky, Lear was a king who did not learn what it is to be a man until he was an *old* man, too old to survive the education in humanity that he and the audience had undergone. He, however, was released from "the rack of this tough world," caught up in his final dream of reunion with Cordelia. I was among the survivors. Yet for days this production left me feeling glad to be alive and half Lear's age.

As You Like It, ROYAL SHAKESPEARE THEATRE COMPANY, LONDON, 1962

If as a spectator I am Shakespeare's creature, he allows me a generous measure of free will. With whom should I identify? That is largely as I like it. Since dramatic life is so generally distributed in his plays, I can at will become a hero, a villain, a god, an innocent bystander. The possibilities of vicarious experience without shame or responsibility seem limitless. In the tragedies, for instance, I can take the lives not only of enemies but of friends, wives, and children, killing deliberately or accidentally, in cold blood or hot, directly or indirectly, by poison, sword, or smothering. Or I can experience suicide. Perhaps the rarest privilege tragedy affords is the opportunity to die more than once.

How involved or detached should I be? That too is for the most part as I like it. Always Shakespeare allows latitudes, just as he does with himself in adapting his source materials and with his actors in interpreting his roles. Is Macbeth mad at the end? Shakespeare explicitly provides an option: "Some say he's mad; others that lesser hate him/ Do call it valiant fury." His text is a deck of cards from which its interpreter may deal out the hand he chooses. It provides thus the scenario for not merely one spectator experience but a whole range of them.

The hand that this production dealt ran heavily to hearts. I was invited to fall as many fathoms-deep in love with Vanessa Redgrave's Rosalind as she did with Orlando. Indulgence was the word. Every character was taken at his own estimate, even Orlando. When Rosalind grieved to see him "wear thy heart in a scarf," his reply—"It is my arm"—was not that of the athletic booby he often seems but of a goodhearted stalwart, gently indicating that it was time now to cut the kidding. Shakespeare made either possibility available. Jaques may be either a profoundly melancholy philosopher (as here) or a sour blowhard. Either is "right." Which is best? The criterion must be: given a certain company of performers and a certain audience, what produces the liveliest play of response?—the fullest, richest, freshest Happening between the performance and its spectators?

Hamlet, STARRING RICHARD BURTON, COLUMBIA
RECORDING

Most interpreters serve up very thin slices from Shakespeare's great feast. To listen to the various recordings of *Hamlet* is to have the feeling of starving in the midst of plenty. Of the numerous possible voices of Hamlet, few performers use more than three or four. The spectator who would hear something like the range of Shakespeare's creation must put together a composite: Olivier's monotone melancholy, Barrymore's neurotic self-disgust, Redgrave's manly resolution, Scofield's antic chirp, Robert Eddison's trembling sensitivity, Forbes-Robertson's hearty geniality, Anew McMaster's volatility, Beerbohm Tree's mournfulness, Gielgud's ringing passion.

Of them all, Richard Burton covers the widest range, yet in such a way as to become a fault. Compare his reading of the first soliloquy with Gielgud's 1934 version. Gielgud builds brilliantly to the climactic phrase "married with my uncle." In fact, his reading is too controlled for so distraught a speech. Burton is at the other extreme. If Gielgud offers architecture, Burton offers fireworks. He plays every line for all it is worth, whether he is praying, cursing, or sobbing. He is most convincing when most bitter. Yet the total effect lacks definition and emphasis, shooting off in so many directions that it often becomes, in Burton's phrase, "Shakespearean noise."

Hamlet, NEW YORK PUBLIC THEATER, 1968

Of course, there are limits to the possibilities that Shakespeare allows. Contrary to a current view, Claudius cannot be taken as a King of Hearts (although at first he may seem to be), nor Hamlet as simply a Knave of Spades. Usually the most dramatic life is to be found within the locus of alternatives Shakespeare permits, and interpreters who go beyond these limits do so at their own risk.

Joe Papp often ran that risk in this adaptation. Take the role assigned to the spectator. If Shakespeare's ideal spectator is

more active than is usual in a modern theater, Papp's is so active
as to be brought onstage to shoot the prince. Yet what resulted
the night I saw it was not so much a superactive spectator as yet
another actor—and not a very good or willing one.

If Papp went too far in this respect, for the most part he did
not go far enough. For instance, he made the set and the whole
theater into a prison. So far so good: Denmark's a prison, in
which there are many confines, wards, and dungeons. But to trap
the spectator in a single dominant Environment throughout, as
Papp did, is the way of a Peter Weiss (in the madhouse of
Marat/Sade) or a Ben Jonson (in *Bartholomew Fair*). Shakespeare's way with an Environment is subtler (we share a mid-
summer night's dream or a twelfth-night revel) and more flexi-
ble: Elsinore is not only a prison but an unweeded garden, a
stage, a bedroom, a grave.

Othello, THE NATIONAL THEATER, CHICHESTER,
ENGLAND, 1964

One might expect that critical readings of Shakespeare's text
would suggest the widest range of spectator response, unfettered
by particular actors or stages. In actuality they usually seem to
me more confining than productions. That is because most readings take a director's point of view, with its proclivity for selec-
tion, intensity, abstraction, and consistency (correspondingly,
the director's verbal "interpretation" is now a staple of theater
programs). They both aspire to the Word, to the neglect of the
varied Incarnation which the actor performs.

Olivier largely follows the modern unheroic reading of the

role of Othello. Every appealing quality is deeply qualified. Clearly this commander fetched his life and being from men of royal siege, yet there is a complacency about his authority, as he stands flaunting one hip, that is hateful. Physically, his strength and grace are undercut by a sensuality that forecasts the gross- ness of his fit. His grief for Desdemona's supposed infidelity— as when he croons "The pity of it" in high falsetto—is nine parts self-pity. Moreover, in each of these qualities is a damaging self- consciousness—the new husband enters smelling a rose, the loung- ing giant's feet are bare but manicured, the general-of-the-hour looks all around the Duke's court for approbation of his poise under fire.

Yet Olivier's Othello produces a much richer spectator ex- perience than does F. R. Leavis' essay (quoted at length in the National Theater program). As I read Leavis I can only feel pitying contempt for Othello's self-deluding folly and revulsion toward his "obtuse and brutal egoism." Olivier's interpretation goes beyond Leavis to make me feel sympathy, even admiration, for this Othello, with all his faults. For I have to admire his courage: the greathearted all-outness of his responses, his utterly vulnerable disregard of the self-protection that lay in restraint. In the same way, for all the excesses of Olivier's own portrayal I cannot help but admire its all-outness.

Henry V, STRATFORD FESTIVAL, ONTARIO, CANADA, 1966

The fullest spectator experiences seem to come from the dramatic interaction of the director's point of view and the actor's. The

Ontario *Henry V* is another case in point. As his program note confirms, director Michael Langham intended a disenchanted reading of the text, along the lines of Harold Goddard, with Henry shown up as an unfeeling opportunist, making a "convenient crusade" against France. To the benefit of the spectator, Langham only partly succeeded. Douglas Rain's Henry was much more than a hollow success. There was no missing Henry's faults: on his orders, and over the silent remonstrances of his noblemen, his French prisoners were slaughtered onstage; his sanctimonious thanks to God after Agincourt were undercut by his nobles' knowing smiles; his practical joke on Williams was carried through, even though his subject was badly wounded in one leg. Yet these failings seemed to me precisely to reveal his humanity, the overtaxed man behind the official image. His manipulations of that image, and his sacrifice of his former cronies to it, seemed a mark of maturity rather than simple hypocrisy: private vices but public virtues, manly recognition of a fact of life, a necessity of rule. In short, Langham plus Rain added up to that rare thing, a hero-politician.

Hamlet, ROYAL SHAKESPEARE THEATRE COMPANY, STRATFORD-UPON-AVON, ENGLAND, 1966

The director addresses me mind to mind, as one contemporary to another; the actor addresses me face to face, as one human being to another.

In his program essay, Peter Hall sees *Hamlet* as being "about the disillusionment which produces an apathy of the will so deep that commitment to politics, to religion or to life is impossible."

This view of the play, and its contemporary relevance, is certainly projected in David Warner's Hamlet, with his long hair and casual manner. But beneath it is the story that Warner regularly enacts (as Henry VI, as Morgan, as Andrew Aguecheek): that of a likable boy who finds himself in a man's plight yet won't grow up. The production's most memorable stage pictures also had to do with the universals of maturation: King Hamlet (a giant mannikin) towering over his son and enfolding him in his arms; Hamlet curling in a fetal position beside his mother on her bed. This Hamlet remained engagingly juvenile to the end, even to his curtain calls—as he pretended surprise at the applause.

JOHN RUSSELL BROWN, "LAUGHTER IN THE LAST PLAYS," *Shakespeare's Plays in Performance* (LONDON, 1967)

Even more than a director, the interpretive commentator tends to address his audience mind to mind. Yet he need not be bound to a director's perspective. John Russell Brown's essay illustrates the value of including as well the perspectives of the actor and the spectator. In his discussion of *The Winter's Tale*, for example, he starts with Tillyard's directorly summary of the play as presenting "the whole tragic pattern from prosperity to destruction, regeneration, and still fairer prosperity." He then analyzes the role of Autolycus, a character who, as Brown remarks, has received "only passing recognition" from literary critics. Drawing on various actors' interpretations, he points out the opportunities for clowning which the part affords and the changes these ring on Tillyard's pattern. Especially, he observes the intimate interplay between fantasy and comedy and the way Autolycus' resilient humor disposes the audience to accept the wonders of the final scene; for "laughter and dreams alike release our fantasies from the restrictive control of our censoring minds." Thus Brown enlarges the spectator's range of appropriate response beyond that of Tillyard and his followers: "The total solemnity of much criticism of the last plays that is current today would strike Elizabethans and Jacobeans as pompous and restrictive. Romance, for them, spelt wonder, delight, *and* mirth."

To arrive at his own fullest response, the reader of a play by Shakespeare should also include all three perspectives. In fact, in his imagination he should work on his own response through the whole process of performing the play. Having read it through as a closet drama, enjoying its plot and language, he should study it as a director would, locating its main lines of interest and appeal, following the largest over-all patterns—its parallel characters, situations, images. Many readers and commentators stop here. But the most responsive reader will go on to rehearse the play in his mind, considering the text in detail as an actor would, hearing and seeing each moment. Not many commentators write from this point of view (A. C. Bradley is one of the few who might be accused of being too actorly in his approach).

At this point the reader will become aware of a disconcerting change in his sense of Shakespeare's presence. As a director, he will have had a strong feeling of being in unmediated touch with the author's purposes and "message." As an actor, he will find that this feeling widens and fades. For he will be constantly conscious of the alternatives among which he must choose. The text will now seem more a kaleidoscope than a single dramatic vision.

The reader should then proceed to perform in the theater of his mind the play as he has interpreted it, playing fully and freely the role as spectator that Shakespeare has assigned him. He should perhaps set aside an afternoon for the purpose, and run his imagined production through at a sitting. At this phase his sense of Shakespeare's control will be most complete. He will understand that the playwright includes his interpreters and spectators within the whole dramatic event he is creating, as still further rings of his enormous circus. From commentaries I would guess that very few readers of Shakespeare persevere to become not only their own directors and actors but their own spectators. Yet that may be the ultimate reward his plays provide.

A SHAKESPEAREAN SPECTATOR

plays Adam to Shakespeare's God.

For the time of the play he becomes a Shakespearean character. His role is like that of any other major Shakespearean character: rounded and multifaceted rather than flat; open to interpretation rather than fixed; developing rather than static.

As such he participates integrally in the life of the play—an experience he approaches with some fear and trembling. For the resulting charge of vitality can be overwhelming: Milton felt turned to marble "with too much conceiving"; Keats "burned" like a phoenix.

Before and beyond anything else, he regards the dramatic event as an experience, a unique "play" of interaction between the script, the performers, and the spectators. Often his own experience will parallel that of the characters: Shakespeare invites him to pity Prospero just as Prospero has come to pity others.

Like the characters, he tries to understand his experience and may come closer than they to doing so. But he does not expect wholly to pluck out the heart of its mystery. In fact, he accepts his search for meaning as part of his experience, going on during as well as after it. Like Hamlet, he is throughout the play engaged in a quest for truth.

He resists any tyranny that would black out his independent existence—whether that of a director who has a bright idea, a critical doctrine that would impose a simplified response (like pity and fear), or his own preconceptions. Yet, if he likes the houselights up, he does not seek the spotlight. He is delighted to be a guest of honor at Shakespeare's party and hopes that the performers will be the life of it.

If he comes to the play as a child—open and receptive to the play world and its ways—he leaves it as an adult, educated by his experience and trusting his own matured responses. When he hears dying Brutus say:

> yet in all my life
> I found no man but he was true to me.
> I shall have glory by this losing day
> More than Octavius and Mark Antony . . .

he has the good sense to see Brutus' quixoticism for what it is and the good heart not altogether to condemn it or him. He knows that Shakespeare—as with the best of his characters—respects his freedom, allows and expects him to lead his own life. That may be the chief reason he comes to the play with fear and trembling. He realizes that it is on his humanity that Shakespeare at last depends.

Stephen Booth

ON THE VALUE OF *Hamlet*

IT IS A TRUTH UNIVERSALLY acknowledged that *Hamlet* as we have it—usually in a conservative conflation of the second quarto and first folio texts—is not really *Hamlet*. The very fact that the *Hamlet* we know is an editor-made text has furnished an illusion of firm ground for leaping conclusions that discrepancies between the probable and actual actions, statements, tone, and diction of *Hamlet* are accidents of its transmission. Thus, in much the spirit of editors correcting printer's errors, critics have proposed stage directions by which, for example, Hamlet can overhear the plot to test Polonius' diagnosis of Hamlet's affliction, or by which Hamlet can glimpse Polonius and Claudius actually spying on his interview with Ophelia. Either of these will make sense of Hamlet's improbable raging at Ophelia in iii.i. The difficulty with such presumably corrective emendation is not only in knowing where to stop, but also in knowing whether to start. I hope to demonstrate that almost everything else in the play has, in its particular kind and scale, an improbability comparable to the improbability of the discrepancy between Hamlet's real and expected behavior to Ophelia; for the moment, I mean only to suggest that those of the elements of the text of *Hamlet* that are incontrovertibly accidental may by their presence have led critics to overestimate the distance between the *Hamlet* we have and the prelapsarian *Hamlet* to which they long to return.

I think also that the history of criticism shows us too ready to indulge a not wholly explicable fancy that in *Hamlet* we behold the frustrated and inarticulate Shakespeare furiously wagging his tail in an effort to tell us something, but, as I said before, the accidents of our texts of *Hamlet* and the alluring analogies they father render *Hamlet* more liable to interpretive assistance than even the other plays of Shakespeare. Moreover, *Hamlet* was of course born into the culture of Western Europe, our culture, whose every thought—literary or nonliterary—is shaped by the Platonic presumption that the reality of anything is other than its apparent self. In such a culture it is no wonder that critics prefer the word *meaning* (which implies effort rather than success) to *saying,* and that in turn they would rather talk about what a work *says* or *shows* (both of which suggest the hidden essence bared of the dross of physicality) than talk about what it *does.* Even stylistic critics are most comfortable and acceptable when they reveal that rhythm, syntax, diction, or (and above all) imagery are vehicles for meaning. Among people to whom "It means a lot to me" says "I value it," in a language where *significant* and *valuable* are synonyms, it was all but inevitable that a work with the peculiarities of *Hamlet* should have been treated as a distinguished and yearning failure.

Perhaps the value of *Hamlet* is where it is most measurable, in the degree to which it fulfills one or another of the fixable identities it suggests for itself or that are suggested for it, but I think that before we choose and argue for one of the ideal forms toward which *Hamlet* seems to be moving, and before we attribute its value to an exaggeration of the degree to which it gets there, it is reasonable to talk about what the play *does* do, and to test the suggestion that in a valued play what it does do is what we value. I propose to look at *Hamlet* for what it undeniably is: a succession of actions upon the understanding of an audience. I set my hypothetical audience to watch *Hamlet* in the text edited by Willard Farnham in The Pelican *Shakespeare* (Baltimore, 1957), a text presumably too long to have fitted into the daylight available to a two o'clock performance, but still an approximation of what Shakespeare's company played.

I

The action that the first scene of *Hamlet* takes upon the understanding of its audience is like the action of the whole, and most of the individual actions that make up the whole. The first scene is insistently incoherent and just as insistently coherent. It frustrates and fulfills expectations simultaneously. The challenge and response in the first lines are perfectly predictable sentry-talk, but—as has been well and often observed—the challenger is the wrong man, the relieving sentry and not the one on duty. A similarly faint intellectual uneasiness is provoked when the first personal note in the play sets up expectations that the play then ignores. Francisco says, "For this relief much thanks. 'Tis bitter cold,/ And I am sick at heart" (1.i.8–9). We want to know why he is sick at heart. Several lines later Francisco leaves the stage and is forgotten. The scene continues smoothly as if the audience had never focused on Francisco's heartsickness. Twice in the space of less than a minute the audience has an opportunity to concern itself with a trouble that vanishes from consciousness almost before it is there. The wrong sentry challenges, and the other corrects the oddity instantly. Francisco is sick at heart, but neither he nor Bernardo gives any sign that further comment might be in order. The routine of sentry-go, its special diction, and its commonplaces continue across the audience's momentary tangential journey; the audience returns as if *it* and not the play had wandered. The audience's sensation of being unexpectedly and very slightly out of step is repeated regularly in *Hamlet*.

The first thing an audience in a theater wants to know is why it is in the theater. Even one that, like Shakespeare's audiences for *Richard II* or *Julius Caesar* or *Hamlet*, knows the story being dramatized wants to hear out the familiar terms of the situation and the terms of the particular new dramatization. Audiences want their bearings and expect them to be given. The first thing we see in *Hamlet* is a pair of sentries. The sight of sentries in real life is insignificant, but, when a work of art focuses on sentries, it is usually a sign that what they are guarding is going to be attacked. Thus, the first answer we have to the question "what is this play about?" is "military threat to a castle and a king," and that leads to our first specific question: "what is that threat?" Horatio's first question ("What, has this thing appeared again to-night?" 1.i.21) is to some extent an answer to the audience's question; its terms are not military, but their implications are appropriately threatening. Bernardo then begins elaborate preparations to tell Horatio what the audience must hear if it is ever to be intellectually comfortable in the play. The audience

has slightly adjusted its expectations to accord with a threat that
is vaguely supernatural rather than military, but the metaphor of
assault in which Bernardo prepares to carry the audience further
along its new path of inquiry is pertinent to the one from which
it has just deviated:

> Sit down awhile,
> And let us once again assail your ears,
> That are so fortified against our story,
> What we two nights have seen.   (1.i.30–33)

We are led toward increased knowledge of the new object—the
ghost—in terms appropriate to the one we assumed and have just
abandoned—military assault. Bernardo's metaphor is obviously
pertinent to his occupation as sentinel, but in the metaphor he is
not the defender but the assailant of ears fortified against his
story. As the audience listens, its understanding shifts from one
system of pertinence to another; but each perceptible change in
the direction of our concern or the terms of our thinking is balanced by the repetition of some continuing factor in the scene;
the mind of the audience is in constant but gentle flux, always
shifting but never completely leaving familiar ground.

Everyone onstage sits down to hear Bernardo speak of the
events of the past two nights. The audience is invited to settle
its mind for a long and desired explanation. The construction of
Bernardo's speech suggests that it will go on for a long time; he
takes three lines (1.i.35–38) to arrive at the grammatical subject
of his sentence, and then, as he begins another parenthetical delay in his long journey toward a verb, "the bell then beating
one," *Enter Ghost*. The interrupting action is not a simple inter-

ruption. The description is interrupted by a repetition of the action described. The entrance of the ghost duplicates on a larger scale the kind of mental experience we have had before. It both fulfills and frustrates our expectations: it is what we expect and desire, an action to account for our attention to sentinels; it is unexpected and unwanted, an interruption in the syntactical routine of the exposition that was on its way to fulfilling the same function. While the ghost is on the stage and during the speculation that immediately follows its departure, the futile efforts of Horatio and the sentries (who, as watchers and waiters, have resembled the audience from the start) are like those of the audience in its quest for information. Marcellus' statement about the ghost is a fair comment on the whole scene: " 'Tis gone and will not answer" (1.i.52), and Horatio's "In what particular thought to work I know not" (1.i.67) describes the mental condition evoked in an audience by this particular dramatic presentation of events as well as it does that evoked in the character by the events of the fiction.

Horatio continues from there into the first statement in the play that is responsive to an audience's requirement of an opening scene, an indication of the nature and direction of the play to follow: "But, in the gross and scope of my opinion,/ This bodes some strange eruption to our state" (1.i.68–69). That vague summary of the significance of the ghost is political, but only incidentally so because the audience, which was earlier attuned to political/military considerations, has now given its attention to the ghost. Then, with only the casual preamble of the word *state*, Marcellus asks a question irrelevant to the audience's newly primary concerns, precisely the question that no one asked when the audience first wanted to know why it was watching the sentries, the question about the fictional situation whose answer would have satisfied the audience's earlier question about its own situation: Marcellus asks "Why this same strict and most observant watch/ So nightly toils the subject of the land" (1.i.71–72). Again what we are given is and is not pertinent to our concerns and expectations. This particular variety among the manifestations of simultaneous and equal propriety and impropriety in *Hamlet* occurs over and over again. Throughout the play, the audience gets information or sees action it once wanted only after a new interest has superseded the old. For one example, when Horatio, Bernardo, and Marcellus arrive in the second scene (1.ii.159), they come to do what they promise to do at the end of scene one, where they tell the audience that the way to information about the ghost is through young Hamlet. By the time they arrive "where we shall find him most conveniently," the audience has a new concern—the relation of Claudius to Gertrude and of Hamlet to both. Of course interruptions of one train of thought by the introduction of another are not only common in *Hamlet* but a commonplace of literature in general. However, although the audience's frustrations and the celerity with which it transfers its concern are similar to those of audiences of, say, Dickens, there is the important difference in *Hamlet* that there are no sharp lines of demarcation. In *Hamlet* the audience does not so much shift its focus as come to find its focus shifted.

Again the first scene provides a type of the whole. When Marcellus asks why the guard is so strict, his question is rather more violent than not in its divergence from our concern for the

boding of the ghost. The answer to Marcellus' question, however, quickly pertains to the subject of ours: Horatio's explanation of the political situation depends from actions of "Our last
king,/ Whose image even but now appeared to us" (1.i.80–81),
and his description of the activities of young Fortinbras as "The
source of this our watch" is harnessed to our concern about the
ghost by Bernardo, who says directly, if vaguely, that the political situation is pertinent to the walking of the ghost:

> I think it be no other but e'en so.
> Well may it sort that this portentous figure
> Comes armèd through our watch so like the king
> That was and is the question of these wars.

(1.i.108–11)

Horatio reinforces the relevance of politics to ghosts in a long
speech about supernatural events on the eve of Julius Caesar's
murder. Both these speeches establishing pertinence are good examples of the sort of thing I mean: both seem impertinent digres-
sions, sufficiently so to have been omitted from the folios.

Now for the second time, *Enter Ghost*. The reentrance
after a long and wandering digression is in itself an assertion of
the continuity, constancy, and unity of the scene. Moreover,
the situation into which the ghost reenters is a careful echo of
the one into which it first entered, with the difference that the
promised length of the earlier exposition is fulfilled in the second.
These are the lines surrounding the first entrance; the italics are
mine and indicate words, sounds, and substance echoed later:

Horatio.   *Well, sit we down,*
    And let us hear Bernardo speak of this.

Bernardo. Last night of all,
>   *When yond same s*tar that's *westward* from the pole
>   Had made his course t' illume that part of heaven
>   Where now it burns, Marcellus and myself,
>   The bell then beating one—

Enter Ghost.

Marcellus. Peace, break thee off. *Look where it comes again.*

(1.i.33–40)

Two or three minutes later a similar situation takes shape in words that echo, and in some cases repeat, those at the earlier entrance:

Marcellus. Good now, sit down, and tell me he that knows,
>   *Why this same s*trict and most observant watch,
>   So nightly toils the subject of the land . . .

. . . .

Enter Ghost

>   *But soft, behold, lo where it comes again!*

(1.i.70–72, 126)

After the ghost departs on the crowing of the cock, the conversation, already extravagant and erring before the second apparition when it ranged from Danish history into Roman, meanders into a seemingly gratuitous preoccupation with the demonology of cocks (1.i.148–65). Then—into a scene that has from the irregularly regular entrance of the two sentinels been a succession of simultaneously expected and unexpected entrances—enters "the morn in russet mantle clad," bringing a great change from darkness to light, from the unknown and unnatural to the known and natural, but also presenting itself personified as another walker, one obviously relevant to the situation and to the dis-

cussion of crowing cocks, and one described in subdued but
manifold echoes of the two entrances of the ghost. Notice particularly the multitude of different kinds of relationship in which
"yon high eastward hill" echoes "yond same star that's westward
from the pole":

> *But look,* the morn in russet mantle clad
> Walks o'er the dew of *yon high eastward* hill.
> *Break we* our watch up . . . .   (1.i.166–68)

The three speeches (1.i.148–73—Horatio's on the behavior of
ghosts at cockcrow, Marcellus' on cocks at Christmas time, and
Horatio's on the dawn) have four major elements running
through them: cocks, spirits, sunrise, and the presence or absence of speech. All four are not present all the time, but the
speeches have a sound of interconnection and relevance to one
another. This at the same time that the substance of Marcellus'
speech on Christmas is just as urgently irrelevant to the concerns
of the scene. As a gratuitous discussion of Christianity, apparently linked to its context only by an accident of poulterer's
lore, it is particularly irrelevant to the moral limits usual to revenge tragedy. The sequence of these last speeches is like the
whole scene and the play in being both coherent and incoherent.
Watching and comprehending the scene is an intellectual triumph for its audience. From sentence to sentence, from event to
event, as the scene goes on it makes the mind of its audience
capable of containing materials that seem always about to fly
apart. The scene gives its audience a temporary and modest but
real experience of being a superhumanly capable mental athlete.
The whole play is like that.

During the first scene of *Hamlet* two things are threatened, one in the play, and one by the play. Throughout the scene the characters look at all threats as threats to the state, and specifically to the reigning king. As the king is threatened *in* scene one, so is the audience's understanding threatened *by* scene one. The audience wants some solid information about what is going on in this play. Scene one is set in the dark, and it leaves the audience in the dark. The first things the play teaches us to value are the order embodied in the king and the rational sureness, purpose, and order that the play as a play lacks in its first scene. Scene two presents both the desired orders at once and in one—the king, whose name even in scene one was not only synonymous with order but was the regular sign by which order was reasserted: the first confusion—who should challenge whom—was resolved in line three by "Long live the king"; and at the entrance of Horatio and Marcellus, rightness and regularity were vouched for by "Friends to this ground. And liegemen to the Dane." As scene two begins it is everything the audience wanted most in scene one. Here it is daylight, everything is clear, everything is systematic. Unlike scene one, this scene is physically orderly; it begins with a royal procession, businesslike and unmistakable in its identity. Unlike the first scene, the second gives the audience all the information it could desire, and gives it neatly. The direct source of both information and orderliness is Claudius, who addresses himself one by one to the groups on the stage and to the problems of the realm, punctuating the units both with little statements of conclusion like "For all, our thanks" and "So much for him" (1.ii.16, 25), and with the word "now" (1.ii.17, 26, 42, 64), by which he signals each remove to a

new listener and topic. Denmark and the play are both now orderly, and are so because of the king. In its specifics, scene two
is the opposite of scene one. Moreover, where scene one presented an incoherent surface whose underlying coherence is only
faintly felt, this scene is the opposite. In scene one the action
taken *by* the scene—it makes its audience perceive diffusion and
fusion, division and unification, difference and likeness at once—
is only an incidental element in the action taken or discussed *in*
the scene—the guards have trouble recognizing each other; the
defense preparation "does not divide the Sunday from the
week," and makes "the night joint-laborer with the day" (1.i.76,
78). In scene two the first subject taken up by Claudius, and the
subject of first importance to Hamlet, is itself an instance of improbable unification—the unnatural natural union of Claudius
and Gertrude. Where scene one brought its audience to feel coherence in incoherence by response to systems of organization
other than those of logical or narrative sequence, scene two
brings its audience to think of actions and characters alternately
and sometimes nearly simultaneously in systems of value whose
contradictory judgments rarely collide in the mind of an audience. From an uneasiness prompted by a sense of lack of order,
unity, coherence, and continuity, we have progressed to an
uneasiness prompted by a sense of their excess.

Claudius is everything the audience most valued in scene
one, but he is also and at once contemptible. His first sentences
are unifications in which his discretion overwhelms things whose
natures are oppugnant. The simple but contorted statement,
"therefore our . . . sister . . . have we . . . taken to wife," takes
Claudius more than six lines to say; it is plastered together with

a succession of subordinate unnatural unions made smooth by
rhythm, alliteration, assonance, and syntactical balance:

> Therefore our sometime sister, now our queen,
> Th' imperial jointress to this warlike state,
> Have we, as 'twere with a defeated joy,
> With an auspicious and a dropping eye,
> With mirth in funeral and with dirge in marriage,
> In equal scale weighing delight and dole,
> Taken to wife.   (I.ii.8–14)

What he says is overly orderly. The rhythms and rhetoric by
which he connects any contraries, moral or otherwise, are too
smooth. Look at the complex phonetic equation that gives a
sound of decorousness to the moral indecorum of "With mirth
in funeral and with dirge in marriage." Claudius uses syntactical
and rhetorical devices for equation by balance—as one would a
particularly heavy and greasy cosmetic—to smooth over any inconsistencies whatsoever. Even his incidental diction is of join-
ing: "jointress," "disjoint," "Colleaguèd" (I.ii.9, 20, 21). The
excessively lubricated rhetoric by which Claudius makes unnatural connections between moral contraries is as gross and
sweaty as the incestuous marriage itself. The audience has double and contrary responses to Claudius, the unifier of contraries.

Scene two presents still another kind of double understanding in double frames of reference. Claudius is the primary figure
in the hierarchy depicted—he is the king; he is also the character
upon whom all the other characters focus their attention; he does
most of the talking. An audience focuses its attention on him. On
the other hand, one of the members of the royal procession was

dressed all in black—a revenger to go with the presumably venge-
ful ghost in scene one. Moreover, the man in black is probably
also the most famous actor in England (or at least of the company). The particulars of the scene make Claudius the focal figure, the genre and the particulars of a given performance focus
the audience's attention on Hamlet.

When the two focuses come together ("But now, my
cousin Hamlet, and my son—") Hamlet's reply (1.ii.65) is
spoken not to the king but to the audience. "A little more
than kin, and less than kind" is the first thing spoken by Hamlet
and the first thing spoken aside to the audience. With that line
Hamlet takes the audience for his own, and gives himself to the
audience as its agent on the stage. Hamlet and the audience are
from this point in the play more firmly united than any other
such pair in Shakespeare, and perhaps in dramatic literature.

Claudius' "my cousin Hamlet, and my son" is typical of his
stylistic unifications of mutually exclusive contrary ideas (cousin,
son). Hamlet's reply does not unify ideas, but disunifies them
(more than kin, less than kind). However, the style in which
Hamlet distinguishes is a caricature of Claudius' equations by
rhetorical balance; here again, what interrupts the order, threatens coherence, and is strikingly at odds with its preamble is also
a continuation by echo of what went before. Hamlet's parody
of Claudius and his refusal to be folded into Claudius' rhetorical
blanket is satisfying to an audience in need of assurance that it is
not alone in its uneasiness at Claudius' rhetoric. On the other
hand, the orderliness that the audience valued in scene two is
abruptly destroyed by Hamlet's reply. At the moment Hamlet
speaks his first line, the audience finds itself the champion of

order in Denmark and in the play, and at the same time irrevocably allied to Hamlet—the one present threat to the order of both.

II

The play persists in taking its audience to the brink of intellectual terror. The mind of the audience is rarely far from the intellectual desperation of Claudius in the prayer scene when the systems in which he values his crown and queen collide with those in which he values his soul and peace of mind. For the duration of *Hamlet* the mind of the audience is as it might be if it could take on, or dared to try to take on, its experience whole, if it dared drop the humanly necessary intellectual crutches of compartmentalization, point of view, definition, and the idea of relevance, if it dared admit any subject for evaluation into any and all the systems of value to which at different times one human mind subscribes. The constant occupation of a sane mind is to choose, establish, and maintain frames of reference for the things of its experience; as the high value placed on artistic unity attests, one of the attractions of art is that it offers a degree of holiday from that occupation. As the creation of a human mind, art comes to its audience ready-fitted to the human mind; it has physical limits or limits of duration; its details are subordinated to one another in a hierarchy of importance. A play guarantees us that we will not have to select a direction for our attention; it offers us isolation from matter and considerations irrelevant to a particular focus or a particular subject. *Hamlet* is more nearly an exception to those rules than other satisfying and bearable works of art. That, perhaps, is the reason so much effort has

gone into interpretations that presume that *Hamlet*, as it is, is
not and was not satisfying and bearable. The subject of literature is often conflict, often conflict of values; but, though the
agonies of decision, knowing, and valuing are often the objects
of an audience's concern, an audience rarely undergoes or even
approaches such agonies itself. That it should enjoy doing so
seems unlikely, but in *Hamlet* the problems the audience thinks
about and the intellectual action of thinking about them are very
similar. *Hamlet* is the tragedy of an audience that cannot make
up its mind.

One of the most efficient, reliable, and usual guarantees of
isolation is genre. The appearance of a ghost in scene one suggests that the play will be a revenge tragedy. *Hamlet* does indeed turn out to be a revenge tragedy, but here genre does not
provide the limited frame of reference that the revenge genre
and genres in general usually establish. The archetypal revenge
play is *The Spanish Tragedy*. In the first scene of that, a ghost
and a personification, Revenge, walk out on the stage and spend
a whole scene saying who they are, where they are, why they
are there, what has happened, and what will happen. The ghost
in *The Spanish Tragedy* gives more information in the first five
lines of the play than there is in the whole first scene of *Hamlet*.
In *The Spanish Tragedy* the ghost and Revenge act as a chorus
for the play. They keep the doubt and turmoil of the characters
from ever transferring themselves to the audience. They keep
the audience safe from doubt, safely outside the action, looking
on. In *The Spanish Tragedy* the act of revenge is presented as a
moral necessity, just as, say, shooting the villain may be in a
Western. Revenge plays were written by Christians and played

to Christian audiences. Similarly, traditional American Westerns were written by and for believers faithful to the principles of the Constitution of the United States. The possibility that an audience's Christian belief that vengeance belongs only to God will color its understanding of revenge in *The Spanish Tragedy* is as unlikely as a modern film audience's consideration of a villain's civil rights when somebody shouts, "Head him off at the pass." The tension between revenge morality and the audience's own Christian morality was a source of vitality always *available* to Kyd and his followers, but one that they did not avail themselves of. Where they did not ignore moralities foreign to the vaguely Senecan ethic of the genre, they took steps to take the life out of conflicts between contrary systems of value.

When Christian morality invades a revenge play, as it does in III.xiii of *The Spanish Tragedy* when Hieronimo says *Vindicta Mihi* and then further echoes St. Paul's "Vengeance is mine; I will repay, saith the Lord," the quickly watered-down Christian position and the contrary position for which Hieronimo rejects it are presented as isolated categories between which the *character* must and does choose. The conflict is restricted to the stage and removed from the mind of the audience. The effect is not to make the contrariety of values a part of the audience's experience but to dispel the value system foreign to the genre, to file it away as, for the duration of the play, a dead issue. In its operations upon an audience of *The Spanish Tragedy*, the introduction and rejection of the Christian view of vengeance is roughly comparable to the hundreds of exchanges in hundreds of Westerns where the new schoolmarm says that the hero should go to the sheriff rather than try to outdraw the villain.

The hero rarely gives an intellectually satisfying reason for taking the law into his own hands, but the mere fact that the pertinent moral alternative has been mentioned and rejected is ordinarily sufficient to allow the audience to join the hero in his morality without fear of further interruption from its own.

The audience of *Hamlet* is not allowed the intellectual comfort of isolation in the one system of values appropriate to the genre. In *Hamlet* the Christian context for valuing is persistently present. In I.v the ghost makes a standard revenge-tragedy statement of Hamlet's moral obligation to kill Claudius. The audience is quite ready to think in that frame of reference and does so. The ghost then—in the same breath—opens the audience's mind to the frame of reference least compatible with the genre. When he forbids vengeance upon Gertrude, he does so in specifically Christian terms: "Taint not thy mind, nor let thy soul contrive/ Against thy mother aught. Leave her to heaven . . ." (I.v.85–86). Moreover, this ghost is at least as concerned that he lost the chance to confess before he died as he is that he lost his life at all.

Most of the time contradictory values do not collide in the audience's consciousness, but the topic of revenge is far from the only instance in which they live anxiously close to one another, so close to one another that, although the audience is not shaken in its faith in either of a pair of conflicting values, its mind remains in the uneasy state common in nonartistic experience but unusual for audiences of plays. The best example is the audience's thinking about suicide during *Hamlet*. The first mention of suicide comes already set into a Christian frame of reference by the clause in which self-slaughter is mentioned: "Or that the Everlasting had not fixed/ His canon 'gainst self-slaughter" (I.ii.131–

32). In the course of the play, however, an audience evaluates suicide in all the different systems available to minds outside the comfortable limitations of art; from time to time in the play the audience thinks of suicide variously as (1) cause for damnation, (2) a heroic and generous action, (3) a cowardly action, and (4) a last sure way to peace. The audience moves from one to another system of values with a rapidity that human faith in the rational constancy of the human mind makes seem impossible. Look, for example, at the travels of the mind that listens to and understands what goes on between the specifically Christian death of Laertes (*Laertes:* ". . . Mine and my father's death come not upon thee,/ Nor thine on me."—*Hamlet:* "Heaven make thee free of it" v.ii.319–21) and the specifically Christian death of Hamlet (*Horatio:* ". . . Good night, sweet prince,/ And flights of angels sing thee to thy rest . . ." v.ii.348–48). During the intervening thirty lines the audience and the characters move from the Christian context in which Laertes' soul departs, into the familiar literary context where they can take Horatio's attempted suicide as the generous and heroic act it is (v.ii.324–31). Audience and characters have likewise no difficulty at all in understanding and accepting the label "felicity" for the destination of the suicide—even though Hamlet, the speaker of "Absent thee from felicity awhile" (v.ii.336), prefaces the statement with an incidental "By heaven (v.ii.332), and even though Hamlet and the audience have spent a lot of time during the preceding three hours actively considering the extent to which a suicide's journey to "the undiscovered country" can be called "felicity" or predicted at all. When "Good night, sweet prince" is spoken by the antique Roman of twenty lines before, both he and the audience return to thinking in a Christian frame of reference, as if they had never been away.

The audience is undisturbed by a nearly endless supply of similar inconstancies in itself and the play; these are a few instances:

The same audience that scorned pretense when Hamlet knew not "seems" in i.ii admires his skill at pretense and detection in the next two acts.

The audience joins Hamlet both in admiration for the self-control by which the player "could force his soul so to his own conceit" that he could cry for Hecuba (ii.ii.537), and in admiration for the very different self-control of Horatio (iii.ii.51–71).

The audience, which presumably could not bear to see a literary hero stab an unarmed man at prayer, sees the justice of Hamlet's self-accusations of delay. The audience also agrees with the ghost when both have a full view of the corpse of Polonius, and when the ghost's diction is an active reminder of the weapon by which Hamlet has just attempted the acting of the dread command: "Do not forget. This visitation/ Is but to whet thy almost blunted purpose" (iii.iv.111–12).

The audience that sees the ghost and hears about its prison house in i.v also accepts the just as obvious truth of "the undiscovered country from whose bourn no traveller returns. . . ."

What have come to be recognized as the problems of *Hamlet* arise at points where an audience's contrary responses come to consciousness. They are made bearable in performance (though not in recollection) by means similar to those by which the audience is carried across the quieter crises of scene one. In performance, at least, the play gives its audience strength and

courage not only to flirt with the frailty of its own understanding but actually to survive conscious experiences of the Polonian
foolishness of faith that things will follow only the rules of the
particular logic in which we expect to see them. The best example of the audience's endurance of self-knowledge is its experiences of Hamlet's madness. In the last moments of Act I Hamlet
makes Horatio, Marcellus, and the audience privy to his intention to pretend madness: ". . . How strange or odd some'er I
bear myself/ (As I perchance hereafter shall think meet/ To
put an antic disposition on) . . ." (I.v.170–73). The audience
sets out into Act II knowing what Hamlet knows, knowing
Hamlet's plans, and secure in its superiority to the characters
who do not. (Usually an audience is superior to the central
characters: it knows that Desdemona is innocent, Othello does
not; it knows what it would do when Lear foolishly divides his
kingdom; it knows how Birnam Wood came to come to Dunsi-
nane. In *Hamlet*, however, the audience never knows what it
would have done in Hamlet's situation; in fact, since the King's
successful plot in the duel with Laertes changes Hamlet's situation so that he becomes as much the avenger of his own death
as of his father's, the audience never knows what Hamlet would
have done. Except for brief periods near the end of the play,
the audience never has insight or knowledge superior to Hamlet's or, indeed, different from Hamlet's. Instead of having superiority *to* Hamlet, the audience goes into the second act to
share the superiority *of* Hamlet.) The audience knows that
Hamlet will play mad, and its expectations are quickly con-
firmed. Just seventy-five lines into Act II, Ophelia comes in and
describes a kind of behavior in Hamlet that sounds like the be-

havior of a young man of limited theatrical ability who is pretending to be mad (ii.i.77–84). Our confidence that this behavior so puzzling to others is well within our grasp is strengthened by the reminder of the ghost, the immediate cause of the promised pretense, in Ophelia's comparison of Hamlet to a creature "loosèd out of hell/ To speak of horrors."

Before Ophelia's entrance, ii.i has presented an example of the baseness and foolishness of Polonius, the character upon whom both the audience and Hamlet exercise their superiority throughout Act ii. Polonius seems base because he is arranging to spy on Laertes. He instructs his spy in ways to use the "bait of falsehood"—to find out directions by indirections (ii.i.1–74). He is so sure that he knows everything, and so sure that his petty scheme is not only foolproof but brilliant, that he is as contemptible mentally as he is morally. The audience laughs at him because he loses his train of thought in pompous byways, so that, eventually, he forgets what he set out to say: "What was I about to say? . . . I was about to say something! Where did I leave?" (ii.i.50–51). When Ophelia reports Hamlet's behavior, Polonius takes what is apparently Hamlet's bait: "Mad for thy love?" (ii.i.85). He also thinks of (and then spends the rest of the act finding evidence for) a specific cause for Hamlet's madness: he is mad for love of Ophelia. The audience knows (1) Hamlet will pretend madness, (2) Polonius is a fool, and (3) what is actually bothering Hamlet. Through the rest of the act, the audience laughs at Polonius for being fooled by Hamlet. It continues to laugh at Polonius' inability to keep his mind on a track (ii.ii.85–130); it also laughs at him for the opposite fault—

he has a one-track mind and sees anything and everything as evidence that Hamlet is mad for love (II.ii.173–212; 394–402). Hamlet, whom the audience knows and understands, spends a good part of the rest of the scene making Polonius demonstrate his foolishness.

Then, in Act III, scene one, the wise audience and the foolish Polonius both become lawful espials of Hamlet's meeting with Ophelia. Ophelia says that Hamlet made her believe he loved her. Hamlet's reply might just as well be delivered by the play to the audience: "You should not have believed me . . ." (III.i.117). In his next speech Hamlet appears suddenly, inexplicably, violently, and really mad—this before an audience whose chief identity for the last hour has consisted in its knowledge that Hamlet is only pretending. The audience finds itself guilty of Polonius' foolish confidence in predictable trains of events. It is presented with evidence for thinking just what it has considered other minds foolish for thinking—that Hamlet is mad, mad for love of an inconstant girl who has betrayed him. Polonius and the audience are the self-conscious and prideful knowers and understanders in the play. They both overestimate the degree of safety they have as innocent onlookers.

When Hamlet seems suddenly mad, the audience is likely for a minute to think that it is mad or that the play is mad. That happens several times in the course of the play; and the play helps audiences toward the decision that the trouble is in themselves. Each time the play seems insane, it also is obviously ordered, orderly, all of a piece. For example, in the case of Hamlet's truly odd behavior with Ophelia in III.i some of the stuff of his speeches to her has been otherwise applied but nonetheless present in the play before (fickleness, cosmetics). Furthermore, after the fact, the play often tells us how we should have reacted; here the King sums up the results of the Ophelia experiment as if they were exactly what the audience expected they would be (which is exactly what they were not): "Love? his affections do not that way tend,/ . . . what he spoke . . ./ Was not like madness" (III.i.162–64). In the next scene, Hamlet enters perfectly sane, and lecturing, oddly enough, on what a play should be (III.ii.1–42). Whenever the play seems mad it drifts back into focus as if nothing odd had happened. The audience is encouraged to agree with the play that nothing did, to assume (as perhaps for other reasons it should) that its own intellect is inadequate. The audience pulls itself together, and goes on to another crisis of its understanding. Indeed, it had to do so in order to arrive at the crisis of the nunnery speech. At exactly the point where the audience receives the information that makes it so vulnerable to Hamlet's inexplicable behavior in the nunnery scene, the lines about the antic disposition (I.v.170–73) act as a much needed explanation—*after the fact of the audience's discomfort*—of jocular behavior by Hamlet ("Art thou there, truepenny?" "You hear this fellow in the cellarage," "Well said, old mole!" I.v.150–51, 162) that is foreign to his tone and attitude earlier in the scene, and that jars with the expectations aroused by the manner in which he and the play have been treating the ghost. For a moment, the play seems to be the work of a madman. Then Hamlet explains what he *will* do, and the audience is invited to feel lonely in foolishly failing to understand that that was what he was doing before.

III

The kind of experience an audience has of *Hamlet* in its large movements is duplicated—and more easily demonstrated—in the microcosm of its responses to brief passages. For example, the act of following the exchange initiated by Polonius' "What do you read, my Lord?" in ii.ii is similar to the larger experience of coping with the whole career of Hamlet's madness:

Polonius. . . . What do you read, my Lord?
Hamlet. Words, words, words.
Polonius. What is the matter, my lord?
Hamlet. Between who?
Polonius. I mean the matter that you read, my lord.
Hamlet. Slanders, sir, for the satirical rogue says here that old
    men have grey beards, that their faces are wrinkled, their
    eyes purging thick amber and plum-tree gum, and that they
    have a plentiful lack of wit, together with most weak hams.
    All which, sir, though I most powerfully and potently be-
    lieve, yet I hold it not honesty to have it thus set down, for
    you yourself, sir, should be old as I am if, like a crab, you
    could go backward.
Polonius. [aside] Though this be madness, yet there is method
    in't. . . .   (ii.ii.190–204)

The audience is full partner in the first two of Hamlet's comically absolute answers. The first answer is not what the questioner expects, and we laugh at the mental inflexibility that makes Polonius prey to frustration in an answer that takes the question literally rather than as it is customarily meant in simi-lar contexts. In his first question Polonius assumes that what he says will have meaning only within the range appropriate to the context in which he speaks. In his second he acts to limit the frame of reference of the first question, but, because "What is the matter?" is a standard idiom in another context, it further widens the range of reasonable but unexpected understanding. On his third try Polonius achieves a question whose range is as limited as his meaning. The audience—composed of smug initiates in Hamlet's masquerade and companions in his cleverness—expects to revel further in the comic revelation of Polonius' limitations. Hamlet's answer begins by letting us laugh at the discomfiture inherent for Polonius in a list of "slanders" of old men. Because of its usual applications, the word "slander" suggests that what is so labeled is not only painful but untrue. Part of the joke here is that these slanders are true. When Hamlet finishes his list, he seems about to continue in the same vein and to demonstrate his madness by saying something like "All which, sir, though . . . , yet are lies." Instead, a syntactical machine ("though . . . yet"), rhetorical emphasis ("powerfully and potently"), and diction ("believe") suitable for the expected denial are used to admit the truth of the slanders: "All which, sir, though I most powerfully and potently believe, yet I hold it not honesty to have it thus set down, for you yourself, sir. . . ." The speech seems to have given up comic play on objection to slanders on grounds of untruth, and to be about to play from an understanding of "slander" as injurious whether true or not. The syntax of "I hold it not honesty . . . , for" signals that a reason for Hamlet's objections will follow, and—in a context where the relevance of the slanders to Polonius gives pain enough to justify suppression of geriatric commonplaces—"for you yourself, sir" signals the probable general direction of the explanation. So far the audience has followed Hamlet's wit without difficulty from one focus to another, but now the bottom falls out from under the audience's own Polonian assumption, in this case the assumption that Hamlet will pretend madness according to pattern: "for you yourself, sir, should be old as I am if, like a crab, you could go backward." This last is exactly the opposite of what Polonius calls it, this is madness without method.

The audience finds itself trying to hear sense in madness; it suddenly undergoes experience of the fact that Polonius' assumptions about cause and effect in life and language are no more arbitrary and vulnerable than its own. The audience has been where it has known that the idea of sanity is insane, but it is there very briefly; it feels momentarily lonely and lost—as it feels when it has failed to get a joke or when a joke has failed to be funny. The play continues blandly across the gulf. Polonius' comment reflects comically on the effects on him of the general subject of old age; the banter between Hamlet and Polonius picks up again; and Polonius continues his self-confident diagnostic asides to the audience. Moreover, the discussion of Hamlet's reading is enclosed by two passages that have strong nonlogical, nonsignificant likeness to one another in the incidental materials they share—breeding, childbearing, death, and walking:

Hamlet. For if the sun breed maggots in a dead dog, being a good kissing carrion—Have you a daughter?
Polonius. I have, my lord.
Hamlet. Let her not walk i' th' sun. Conception is a blessing, but as your daughter may conceive, friend, look to't.
Polonius. [aside] How say you by that? Still harping on my

daughter. Yet he knew me not at first. 'A said I was a fish-
monger. 'A is far gone, far gone. And truly in my youth I
suffered much extremity for love, very near this. I'll speak
to him again.—What do you read, my lord?

(II.ii.181–90)

Polonius. [aside] Though this be madness, yet there is method
      in't.—Will you walk out of the air, my lord?
Hamlet. Into my grave?
Polonius. Indeed, that's out of the air. [aside] How pregnant
      sometimes his replies are! a happiness that often madness
      hits on, which reason and sanity could not so prosperously
      be delivered of . . . .   (II.ii.203–9)

From beginning to end, in all sizes and kinds of materials,
the play offers its audience an actual and continuing experience
of perceiving a multitude of intense relationships in an equal
multitude of different systems of coherence, systems not subordinated to one another in a hierarchy of relative power. The
way to an answer to "What is so good about *Hamlet*?" may be
in an answer to the same question about its most famous part, the
"To be or not to be" soliloquy.

The soliloquy sets out with ostentatious deliberation, ration-
ality, and precision. Hamlet fixes and limits his subject with authority and—considering that his carefully defined subject takes
in everything humanly conceivable—with remarkable confidence: "To be, or not to be—that is the question." He then re-
states and further defines the question in four lines that echo the
physical proportions of "To be or not to be" (two lines on the
positive, two on the negative) and also echo the previous grammatical construction ("to suffer . . . or to take arms"):

> Whether 'tis nobler in the mind to suffer
> The slings and arrows of outrageous fortune
> Or to take arms against a sea of troubles
> And by opposing end them.
>
> (III.i.57–60)

The speech is determinedly methodical about defining a pair of alternatives that should be as easily distinguishable as any pair imaginable; surely being and not being are distinct from one another. The next sentence continues the pattern of infinitives, but it develops the idea of "not to be" instead of continuing the positive-negative alternation followed before:

> To die, to sleep—
> No more—and by a sleep to say we end
> The heartache, and the thousand natural shocks
> That flesh is heir to. 'Tis a consummation
> Devoutly to be wished.
>
> (III.i.60–64)

As an audience listens to and comprehends the three units "To die," "to sleep," and "No more," some intellectual uneasiness should impinge upon it. "To sleep" is in apposition to "to die," and their equation is usual and perfectly reasonable. However, death and sleep are also a traditional type of unlikeness; they could as well restate "to be or not to be" (to sleep or to die) as "not to be" alone. Moreover, since to die is to sleep, and is also to sleep no more, no vocal emphasis or no amount of editorial punctuation will limit the relationship between "to sleep" and "no more." Thus, when "and by a sleep to say we end . . ." re-asserts the metaphoric equation of death and sleep, the listener feels a sudden and belated need to have heard "no more" as the isolated summary statement attempted by the punctuation of modern texts. What is happening here is that the apparently sure distinction between "to be" and "not to be" is becoming less and less easy to maintain. The process began even in the methodically precise first sentence where passivity to death-dealing slings and arrows described "to be," and the positive aggressive action of taking arms described the negative state, "not to be." Even earlier, the listener experienced a substantially irrelevant instability of relationship when "in the mind" attached first to "nobler," indicating the sphere of the nobility, and then to "suffer," indicating the sphere of the suffering: "nobler in the mind to suffer."

"The thousand natural shocks/ That flesh is heir to" further denies the simplicity of the initial alternatives by opening the mind of the listener to considerations excluded by the isolated question whether it is more pleasant to live or to die; the substance of the phrase is a summary of the pains of life, but its particulars introduce the idea of duty. "Heir" is particularly relevant to the relationship and duty of Hamlet to his father; it also implies a continuation of conditions from generation to generation that is generally antithetical to any assumption of finality in death. The diction of the phrase also carries with it a suggestion of the Christian context in which flesh is heir to the punishment of Adam; the specifically religious word "devoutly" in the next sentence opens the idea of suicide to the Christian ethic from which the narrowed limits of the first sentences had briefly freed it.

While the logical limits and controls of the speech are falling away, its illogical patterns are giving it their own coherence. For example, the constancy of the infinitive construction maintains an impression that the speech is proceeding as methodically as it began; the word "to," in its infinitive use and otherwise, appears thirteen times among the eighty-five words in the first ten lines of the soliloquy. At the same time that the listener is having trouble comprehending the successive contradictions of "To die, to sleep—/ No more—and by a sleep to say we end . . . ," he also hears at the moment of crisis a confirming echo of the first three syllables and the word "end" from "*and by op*posing *end* them" in the first three syllables and word "end" in "*and by a* sleep to say we *end*." As the speech goes on, as it loses more and more of its rational precision, and as "to be" and "not to be" become less and less distinguishable, rhetorical coherence continues in force. The next movement of the speech begins with a direct repetition, in the same metrical position in the line, of the words with which the previous movement began: "To die, to sleep." The new movement seems, as each new movement has seemed, to introduce a restatement of what has gone before; the rhetorical construction of the speech insists that all the speech does is make the distinct natures of "to be" and "not to be" clearer and clearer:

> To die, to sleep—
> To sleep—perchance to dream: ay, there's the rub,
> For in that sleep of death what dreams may come
> When we have shuffled off this mortal coil,
> Must give us pause. There's the respect
> That makes calamity of so long life.

> (III.i.64–69)

As Hamlet describes his increasing difficulty in seeing death as the simple opposite of life, the manner of his description gives his listener an actual experience of that difficulty; "shuffled off this mortal coil" says "cast off the turmoil of this life," but "shuffled off" and "coil" both suggest the rejuvenation of a snake which, having once thrown her enamell'd skin, reveals another just like it underneath. The listener also continues to have difficulty with the simple action of understanding; like the nature of the things discussed, the natures of the sentences change as they are perceived: "what dreams may come" is a common construction for a question, and the line that follows sounds like a subordinate continuation of the question; it is not until we hear "must give us pause" that we discover that "what dreams may come" is a noun phrase, the subject of a declarative sentence that only comes into being with the late appearance of an unexpected verb. In the next sentence ("There's the respect/ That makes calamity of so long life"), logic requires that we understand "makes calamity so long-lived," but our habitual understanding of *makes . . . of* constructions and our recent indoctrination in the pains of life make us likely to hear the contradictory, illogical, and yet appropriate "makes a long life a calamity."

Again, however, the lines sound ordered and reasonable. The rejected first impressions I have just described are immediately followed by a real question, and one that is largely an insistently long list of things that make life a monotonously painful series of calamities. Moreover, nonlogical coherence is provided by the quiet and intricate harmony of "to dream," "of death," and "shuffled off" in the metrical centers of three successive lines; by the echo of the solidly metaphoric "there's the rub" in the vague "there's the respect"; and by the repetition of "for" from "For in that sleep" to begin the next section of the speech.

> For who would bear the whips and scorns of time,
> Th' oppressor's wrong, the proud man's contumely,
> The pangs of despised love, the law's delay,
> The insolence of office, and the spurns
> That patient merit of th' unworthy takes,
> When he himself might his quietus make
> With a bare bodkin? Who would fardels bear,
> To grunt and sweat under a weary life,
> But that the dread of something after death,
> The undiscovered country, from whose bourn
> No traveller returns, puzzles the will,
> And makes us rather bear those ills we have
> Than fly to others that we know not of?
>
> (III.i.70–82)

Although the list in the first question is disjointed and rhythmically frantic, the impression of disorder is countered by the regularity of the definite article, and by the inherently conjunctive action of six possessives. The possessives in 's, the possessives in *of*, and the several nonpossessive *of* constructions are themselves an underlying pattern of simultaneous likeness and difference. So is the illogical pattern present in the idea of burdens, the word "bear," and the word "bare." The line in which the first of these questions ends and the second begins is an epitome of the construction and action of the speech: "With a bare bodkin? Who would fardels bear, ..." The two precisely equal halves of a single rhythmic unit hold together two separate syntactical units. The beginning of the new sentence, "Who would fardels bear," echoes both the beginning, "For who would bear," and the sound of one word, "bare," from the end of the old. Moreover, "bare" and "bear," two words that are both the same and different, participate here in statements of the two undistinguishable alternatives: "to be, or not to be"—to bear fardels, or to kill oneself with a bare bodkin.

The end of the speech sounds like the rationally achieved conclusion of just such a rational investigation as Hamlet began. It begins with *thus*, the sign of logical conclusion, and it gains a sound of inevitable truth and triumphant clarity from the incremental repetition of *and* at the beginning of every other line. The last lines are relevant to Hamlet's behavior in the play at large and therefore have an additional sound of rightness here. Not only are the lines broadly appropriate to the play, the audience's understanding of them is typical of its understanding throughout the play and of its understanding of the previous particulars of this speech: Hamlet has hesitated to kill Claudius. Consideration of suicide has seemed a symptom of that hesitancy. Here the particular from which Hamlet's conclusions about his inability to act derive is his hesitancy to commit suicide. The audience hears those conclusions in the context of his failure to take the action that suicide would avoid.

> Thus conscience does make cowards of us all,
> And thus the native hue of resolution
> Is sicklied o'er with the pale cast of thought,

> And enterprises of great pitch and moment
> With this regard their currents turn awry
> And lose the name of action.

(III.i.83–88)

These last lines are accidentally a compendium of phrases descriptive of the action of the speech and the process of hearing it. The speech puzzles the will, but it makes us capable of facing and bearing puzzlement. The "To be or not to be" soliloquy is a type of the over-all action of *Hamlet*. In addition, a soliloquy in which being and its opposite are indistinguishable is peculiarly appropriate to a play otherwise full of easily distinguishable pairs that are not easily distinguished from one another by characters or audience or both: Rosencrantz and Guildenstern; the pictures of Gertrude's two husbands (III.iv.54–68); the hawk and the handsaw (II.ii.370); and father and mother who are one flesh and so undistinguished in Hamlet's farewell to Claudius (IV.iii.48–51). The soliloquy is above all typical of a play whose last moments enable its audience to look unblinking upon a situation in which Hamlet, the finally successful revenger, is the object of Laertes' revenge; a situation in which Laertes, Hamlet's victim, victimizes Hamlet; a situation in which Fortinbras, the threat to Denmark's future in scene one, is its hope for political salvation; in short, a situation in which any identity can be indistinguishable from its opposite. The soliloquy, the last scene, the first scene, the play—each and together—make an impossible coherence of truths that are both undeniably incompatible and undeniably coexistent.

IV

The kind of criticism I am doing here may be offensive to readers conditioned to think of revelation as the value of literature and the purpose of criticism. The things I have said about *Hamlet* may be made more easily palatable by the memory that illogical coherence—coherent madness—is a regular topic of various characters who listen to Hamlet and Ophelia. In the Reynaldo scene (II.i) and Hamlet's first talk with Rosencrantz and Guildenstern the power of rhetoric and context to make a particular either good or bad at will is also a topic in the play. So too is the perception of clouds which may in a moment look "like a camel indeed," and "like a weasel" and be "very like a whale" (III.ii.361–67).

What I am doing may seem antipoetical; it should not. On the contrary, the effects I have described in *Hamlet* are of the same general kind as the nonsignificant coherences made by rhythm, rhyme, alliteration, and others of the standard devices of prosody. For example, the physics of the relationship among Hamlet, Laertes, Fortinbras, and Pyrrhus, the four avenging sons in *Hamlet*, are in their own scale and substance the same as those of the relationship among *cat, rat, bat,* and *chat.* The theme of suicide, for all the inconstancy of its fluid moral and emotional value, is a constant and unifying factor in the play. So too is the theme of appearance and reality, deceit, pretense, disguise, acting, seeming, and cosmetics which gives the play coherence even though its values are as many as its guises and labels. The analogy of rhyme or of a pair of like-metered lines applies profitably to the nonsignifying relationship between Hamlet's two interviews with women. Both the nunnery scene with Ophelia and the closet scene with Gertrude are stage-managed and overlooked by Polonius; neither lady understands Hamlet; both are amazed by his intensity; in both scenes Hamlet makes a series of abortive departures before his final exit. There is a similar kind of insignificant likeness in numerous repeated patterns of scenes and situations like that of Hamlet's entrance reading in ii.ii and its echo in Ophelia's show of devotional reading in iii.i. Indeed, the same sort of thing can be said about any of the themes and images whose value critics have tried to convert to significance.

The tools of prosody and the phenomena I have talked about show their similarity well when they cooperate in Hamlet's little poem on perception and truth, a poem that is a model of the experience of the whole play. Polonius reads it to the king and queen:

> Doubt thou the stars are fire;
>   Doubt that the sun doth move;
> Doubt truth to be a liar;
>   But never doubt I love.   (ii.ii.116–19)

I suggest that the pleasure of intellectual possession evoked by perception of the likeness and difference of "fire" and "liar" and of "move" and "love," or among the four metrically like and unlike lines, or between the three positive clauses and the one negative one, or between "stars" and "sun" or "truth" and "liar" is of the same kind as the greater achievement of intellectual mastery of the greater challenge presented by "doubt" in the first three lines. The first two *doubts* demand disbelief of two things that common sense cannot but believe. The third, whose likeness to the first two is insisted upon by anaphora, is made unlike them by the words that follow it: disbelief that truth is a liar is a logical necessity; therefore, "doubt" here must mean "believe" or "incline to believe" as it does earlier in this scene (l. 56) and several other times in the play. To be consistent with the pair of hyperbolic impossibilities to which it is coupled, and to fit the standard rhetorical formula (Doubt what cannot be doubted, but do not doubt . . .) in which it appears, "Doubt truth to be a liar" must be understood in a way inconsistent with another pattern of the poem, the previously established meaning of "doubt." Even the first two lines, which seem to fit the hyperbolic formula so well, may make the poem additionally dizzying because their subject matter could remind a Renaissance listener (once disturbed by the reversal of the meaning of the third "doubt") of doubts cast upon common-sense impressions by still recent astronomical discoveries, notably that the diurnal motion of the sun is an illusion.

The urgent rhetorical coherence of the poem is like that of the play. As the multitude of insistent and overlapping systems of coherence in the poem allows its listener to hold the two contradictory meanings of "doubt" in colloid-like suspension and to experience both the actions "doubt" describes, so in the play at large an alliteration of subjects—a sort of rhythm of ideas whose substance may or may not inform the situation dramatized—gives shape and identity, nonphysical substance, to the play that *contains* the situation. Such a container allows Shakespeare to replace *conclusion* with *inclusion;* it provides a particular and temporary context that overcomes the intellectual terror ordinarily inherent in looking at an action in all the value systems it invades. Such a container provides a sense of order and limitation sufficient to replace the comforting boundaries of carefully isolated frames of reference; it makes its audience capable of contemplating more truth than the mind should be able to bear.

In summary I would say that the thing about *Hamlet* that has put Western man into a panic to explain it is not that the play is incoherent, but that it is coherent. There are plenty of incoherent plays; nobody ever looks at them twice. This one, because it obviously makes sense and because it just as obviously cannot be made sense of, threatens our inevitable working assumption that there are no "more things in earth" than can be understood in one philosophy. People see *Hamlet* and tolerate inconsistencies that it does not seem they could bear. Students of the play have explained that such people do not, in fact, find the play bearable at all. They therefore whittle the play down for us to the size of one of its terms, and deny the others. Truth is bigger than any one system for knowing it, and *Hamlet* is bigger than any of the frames of reference it inhabits. *Hamlet* allows us to comprehend—hold on to—all the contradictions it contains. *Hamlet* refuses to cradle its audience's mind in a closed generic framework, or otherwise limit the ideological context of its actions. In *Hamlet* the mind is cradled in nothing more than the fabric of the play. The superior strength and value of that fabric is in the sense it gives that it is unlimited in its range, and that its audience is not only sufficient to comprehend but is in the act of achieving total comprehension of all the perceptions to which its mind can open. The source of the strength is in a rhetorical economy that allows the audience to perform both of the basic

actions of the mind upon almost every conjunction of elements
in the course of the play: it perceives strong likeness, and it perceives strong difference. Every intellectual conjunction is also a
disjunction, and any two things that pull apart contain qualities
that are simultaneously the means of uniting them.

John Russell Brown

THE THEATRICAL ELEMENT OF SHAKESPEARE

CRITICISM

"It has taken more bookish Shakespeareans many generations to understand the controlling importance of stage performance," wrote Harry Levin in *The Question of "Hamlet"* (1959).[1] In his view, criticism has recently made a determined attempt to consider Shakespeare's plays in the theater, as well as on the printed page. I think that this is so, and that persuasion directed to initiating this practice is now unnecessary; at this stage in our approach to Shakespeare's plays, it is more profitable to ask what effect this renewed theatrical consciousness has had.

Levin's own book exemplifies one common way for a critic to remember the theater. Three times he refers to actual performances to demonstrate a critical attitude. Sarah Bernhardt's acting of Hamlet is said to be part of the "romantic legend of a weakling, too delicate for this world" (p. 5). Edwin Booth, identified as "a romantic actor," is held to be typical of those who found "congenial" the assumption that "Hamlet was really

[1] *The Question of "Hamlet"* (Oxford, 1959), pp. 131–32.

the victim of the mental disease he claimed to be simulating" (p. 111). This critic has little time for these notions and his theatrical instances are presented with overtones of ridicule. In support of an attitude that Levin considers more important, a reference to an actor introduces a paragraph and is given a vague puff of recommendation. So Tommaso Salvini, said to be "one of the most celebrated Hamlets of theatrical history," is quoted as being able to sum up this part "in a single trait: *il dubbio*" (p. 74). But having provided the entrance for a new theme, theatrical criticism retires and the paragraph proceeds with a long quotation from Erasmus, who is said to be borrowing from Plato. On each of these three occasions the critic is using particular theatrical references, none too precisely, as a kind of exfoliation of his discourse on the play; they are by no means essential to his purpose.

Far more ambitiously a sensitivity to the theatrical nature of Shakespeare's writings has led critics to look as well as read. On all hands in contemporary criticism we can find attention paid to what happens onstage as well as what is said. For example, the section on *Macbeth* in John Arthos, *The Art of Shakespeare* (1964), opens boldly with the comment:

> The play began with the supernatural in obvious and fascinating theatrical devices, and it ended with as preposterous a one, the fulfilment of the last of the prophecies.
>
> (pp. 36–37)

The usual difficulty is how to make use of such observations: if there is a great deal of spectacular drama, how is that to be related to the verbal life of the play that is finely and allusively explored according to critical methods designed for wholly literary texts? The main argument in this consideration of *Macbeth* in *The Art of Shakespeare* is centered on the words; the eloquent peroration to Arthos' study makes no mention at all of what is seen, of the theater, or of the "preposterous theatricality" of the play.

Attention to the visual elements seems most germane to a critic's purpose when they are minutely related to speech. Again Harry Levin's book exemplifies this. It is divided into four parts, called "Presuppositions," "Interrogation," "Doubt," and "Irony." Its structure, as these headings suggest, is determined by verbal and literary concepts, nothing clearly theatrical or visual. But this is how the critic's mind is based and how it works; it is when his "understanding of the controlling importance of stage performance" is most closely allied to this basic way of thought that it brings greatest interest and illumination; then it seems genuinely necessary to his discourse and not, merely, the means to import individual jewels of theatrical reference.

For example, Levin makes much of the drinking in the last scene of *Hamlet*, relating this activity to the words used earlier in the first court scene (1.ii) and in Hamlet's talk with Horatio before seeing the Ghost. He notices the contrasted actions involved here, so that one reflects on the other and gives definition: Gertrude, he says, "sips" the poisoned drink (p. 98), but Hamlet makes sure of Claudius' "union" by "forcing the cup to his lips." A fourth reference to a particular performance in Levin's book does relate to his interest in specific words, and has the same kind of usefulness. In reading Hamlet's scene with Ophelia the simple words, "I was the more deceived," may well make no more impact than those that come before and after; but Levin reminds us that in these words Mrs. Siddons is "said to have concentrated the essence of her role" as Ophelia (p. 28). Levin believes that doubt is central to the theme of the play, and this theatrical reference helps him to give more than usual importance to a single line.

Levin's book on *Hamlet* shows theatrical understanding working best in step with his basically verbal analysis. Is this as far as the new theatrical criticism should go? Levin himself seems to think so. The quotation with which I began should be continued:

> It has taken more bookish Shakespeareans many generations to understand the controlling importance of stage performance; now that such understanding has been reached, there may be some danger of overemphasis.

Five years after Levin's book, another book on the same play, called *An Approach to "Hamlet,"* was published by L. C. Knights. In this I can find only one theatrical reference. It comes in considering descriptions of the Ghost in Act i, scene i:

> None of this [Knights notes] provides any very clear answer to the question that an audience is likely to ask—What sort of a ghost is this? Is it good or bad?   (p. 44)

The remembrance that this is a play to be performed is a little oblique, and it raises pure supposition: would an audience ask this question? would an audience, gripped or at least led forward by what *is* being said and done on the stage, ask any question at all, particularly if it is not posed in the play? What does chiefly affect the audience's mode of response in this first scene, where do they look, what do they listen for, and how do they do this? These are important considerations, but if a critic wishes to raise them he must do so responsibly, with some care.

No critic writing today could be unaware that some attention has been paid to theatrical matters and, clearly, some have decided not to take this very seriously. Who is right? Is there "some danger of overemphasis"?

I have already implied my own view: I think the "understanding" has not gone far enough. This is not because great revaluations have been effected already, but partly because theatrical criticism has made such little headway. The first critics to take this path with purposeful intention seem to have done the best. We still look back to Granville-Barker, writing as much as forty years ago. If challenged on the usefulness of theatrical criticism, we remember how Granville-Barker vindicated the structure of *Antony and Cleopatra* by pointing to the stage effects of the juxtaposition of short scenes. We think too of his championship of *Love's Labour's Lost* when he showed the theatrical effect of its elaborate language. Yet even here there is no complete vindication of his critical bias: *Antony and Cleopatra* is still considered in much the same critical terms as it was fifty years ago, and recent productions have not shown the play to be any more certain of theatrical conviction; *Love's Labour's Lost* is now established in critical favor, but often for subtleties unnoticed by Granville-Barker. If this early criticism of Shakespeare's plays in a fully theatrical context gives hope, it is of revaluations with limited or temporary relevance.

Yet none of this persuades me that the theatrical course is

ineffective. In the theater everything is subject to revaluation, every time a play is performed; this is the nature of the medium. An assurance that this or that interpretation or mode of performance is the only one that is appropriate to a dramatic text will not come easily; for a start, no mode of performance will be easy to describe. After trying to consider Shakespeare's plays in their theatrical element, I have become almost incapable of "evaluative criticism" in any usual sense of those words. I discover possibilities, forgotten details, unobserved correspondences, potentialities; I open questions and rarely am able to close them. In some conditions of performance, one opinion about Shakespeare's writing and imagination seems useful and, even, correct; but when conditions change that opinion is often discarded.

Among the usual metaphors or analogies used to describe a critic's task, certain ones are dominant. The critic is said to judge, to weigh, to define, to assess or even "fix." He sometimes seems to be "taking sights," or measuring or estimating height, depth, or width. He "looks for a pattern," "plucks out," or "dissects," the "heart of the mystery." He "places" a work of art in a perspective or a background. I see the appropriateness of all these metaphors, but they do not correspond to my basic activity in trying to understand one of Shakespeare's plays in a theatrical context. I am then acutely aware of the temporary nature of every judgment, because each moment of understanding is influenced by many accidental circumstances of embodiment and confrontation. On no two occasions does a play seem the same; it cannot be held still for "examination."

Sculptors sometimes say that a block of marble has a figure within it, waiting to be released. I think a play-text is like that:

there is something that has to be discovered, in three dimensions, in time, sight, sound, words, rhythms. And each sculptor—each actor, director, and theatrical critic—will find a different figure within the living, idiosyncratic block of theatrical raw material. Each time he tackles a play he will make a new start, find a new structure, and unintentionally discard elements that had seemed important before. If the critic's encounter with a play is like that, how can he construct an argument that will establish an inescapable revaluation? If a critic of Shakespeare attempts to "fix" a play, he will do so most readily by ignoring its theatrical element—that is, by wholly unwarranted simplification.

The most obvious way to start considering the theatrical aspects of a Shakespeare play is to study a production of it. But this is easier to say than to do. If the critic detaches his mind at a performance, so that it is free to question, compare, and analyze, the production immediately changes, because the forward pressure of events is lost. The critic must see the same production many times, and ask most of his questions afterwards. Then more problems arise: why did he fail to hear certain words that in reading had seemed highly significant? Going back to check, he may find that they were indeed not spoken by anyone, but were cut from the acting text—why?—or he may discover that they were spoken, but now he wonders why they escaped his notice at first. Questions proliferate: why did certain words sound unusually impressive? why did the empty stage on one particular occasion seem so meaningful? why did the critic look only at one of the many persons onstage? Talking about the performance afterwards with other members of the same audience seldom brings more assurance, for what has taken possession of one imagination may have failed to register with another. The critic will frequently reflect that the production he has seen cannot possibly be like a performance envisaged by Shakespeare; audience, theater, staging, performances, all are very different. He will often be annoyed by what is obviously makeshift or meretricious in the productions he sees.

All this is common experience for anyone who tries to analyze a play in the "understanding of the controlling importance of stage performance." Two courses seem open. One critic will give up, and argue that these accidentally varying emphases come from misunderstanding and irresponsibility in actors and directors—and he should add in audiences—and take us further away from "the words themselves," which is all that Shakespeare has tangibly "left us." Another critic will continue his quest and bring scholarly method to his problem. He will go to still more productions, so that he can compare one with another. He will read all available dramatic criticism in order to check his reactions against others, especially those of theatergoers familiar with theatrical tradition and procedures. He will study the stage history of his chosen play, so that the fashions and predilections of this time and age can be offset by those of previous generations. So this critic will not only gain a historical perspective on any one production but will also be able to give some consideration to those performances that were, in their own time, judged to be preeminently revealing of Shakespeare's achievement.

Such scholarly activity brings rewards. Some elements in audience reaction to a play are consistently present, or almost so; some lines seem particularly memorable, though capable of diverse interpretations. Such facts the critic will collect and consider. He will also become a theater historian, for the evidence of past performances will be more meaningful if he knows the conditions in which the play was staged, the lines that were cut (and added), the habitual manner of individual actors. For example, Harry Levin's reference to Mrs. Siddons would tell us more about the play if we knew the particular kind of power that she possessed as an actress: "when such-and-such a kind of actress is portraying Ophelia," we should say, "these words about deceit can seem tense and weighted with significance."

The critic will now go to the theater himself with more awareness, and he will have opened up many precise considerations. How is the performance governed by casting problems within the company, by the kind of setting used, by the intensity or variability of the lighting? What influence, if any, has the director had over the acting? Do some incidents stand out by accident rather than design, because they are out of style with the rest of the production? Do others disappear because the actors cannot respond to some of the demands of the text, lacking vocal, physical, or emotional resource, or simply by not being aware of them? By this time the critic is in danger of being overwhelmed by his own curiosity, and he will again reconsider his procedures. This time, I think, there are three courses open to him. Again he may give up: he seems to be still further from direct contact with Shakespeare's words, and at this stage has gained only perplexity. Or he will start "working in the theater" for himself, either by taking part in actual productions or else by rehearsing and producing the play in his own mind, in the theater of his mind.

From the beginning of criticism the theater of the mind has attracted attention. In so far as a critic "hears" lines and "sees" actions and gestures, he is staging the play there; Harry Levin must have "staged" the business with the goblets in the last scene of *Hamlet* in his mind. But there is a world of difference between such occasional "realizations" and the difficult and complicated activity which takes place after the critic has given some detailed and prolonged study to actual productions and theater history. For example, is it true to say, with Levin, that Gertrude "sips" from the poisoned chalice? In her brave concern to identify herself with her son in the presence of her second husband, to reassure him, perhaps to reassure everyone and not least herself, would she "sip"? Surely the gesture should be stronger than this word implies. In any case, *when* does she drink: when she says "The queen carouses to thy fortune, Hamlet"? or after Hamlet has said "Good madam"? or while the King says "Gertrude, do not drink"? or after the first or second phrases of her own "I will, my lord; I pray you pardon me"? All these moments give a practical opportunity for the actress to drink, and each will probably suggest a different kind of drinking; each, with the accompanying words, will have a different effect upon the audience's understanding of the play. (I am inclined to think she drinks as early as possible, because one line after the words I have last quoted, Hamlet is ready to say "I dare not drink yet, madam—by and by.") It is one thing to consider the visual effect of this gesture in the theater of the mind, and quite another to relate that to the infinite possibilities and the limiting practicalities of a whole play in performance. Momentary attention to imaginary performance is arguably worse than disregarding it entirely; it is so easy to be pleased with the glimpses caught of possible meanings and possible excitements without proceeding to relate that incident with the complete, continuously changing stage picture and the continuously sustained and developing impersonations.

Even when the critic can begin to work responsibly in the theater of his mind, needing just as much imagination as he did at first, but bringing also a meticulous particularity and a full view of the stage, there are traps in this procedure. The imaginary stage is not easily kept constant in size; it often has no dimensions at all. It has no individual actors, to whom some things are technically impossible and who once onstage cannot be forgotten. It is not controlled by time, but is liable to have several differing and unpredictable clocks so that time goes with varying paces and can often be forgotten entirely. In a word, it is hard to keep one's eye on the object, the full play, in the theater of the mind. Keeping the play in continual rehearsal in this theatre is a stimulating, exploratory, necessary activity; but it is not easily a responsible or scholarly investigation. If he wishes to understand the "controlling importance of stage performance" the critic has no choice: he must also work—in some way—in a "real" theater, no matter how inadequate or how fortuitously contrived. He must meet facts, some facts at least.

I used to think that the critic needed a theatrical laboratory where he could make "research tests" and observe or even measure the effects of different interpretations of the textual evidence. But a fragment of a play suffers out of sequence and out of the

developing context of the whole play in performance. Moreover the contents of the experiment can never be adequately
controlled: individual actors bring with them so much that cannot be fully understood and cannot be discarded; stages, audiences, and ensemble effects are not easily made to measure, even
if the critic-researcher could contrive an adequate measure. The
theater is an art form in which accident and preconditioning
have irradicable influences. They are, indeed, essential ingredients, and their effects over a whole play are endlessly and subtly
revealing.

The theatrical critic will certainly be tempted to change his
mind, to believe that he had been mistaken about the "controlling
importance" of this elusive reality. The words on the printed
page are each fixed there in due sequence of regular type: would
it not be more responsible to concentrate attention on them,
knowing that they are not all the play but, at least, a definite and
significant part of the play? But by this time it is, I find, too late
to turn back. So much has been seen and heard, so many theatrical potentialities of the text have been discovered, that the words
simply will not lie down again, in their original place; once a
play is alive in its theatrical and variable element it will not
easily die. The true choice is not between a verbal reading and
a theatrical one, but whether or not to allow Shakespeare's
words to awaken—to create, as it were, on their own account;
in the theater, which is its element, his text is the originator and
energizer of all that we see and hear.

I think that becoming involved directly, at firsthand, with
the process of a play in rehearsal and performance is an inevitable
step that must be taken by the responsible critic of Shakespeare's
plays. I know this is an extreme view, but for firsthand (if not

original) work, nothing less will do. We accept this in editorial matters: a critic can take his text on trust, making some effort to find out what is the best-regarded edition to use and prefacing his work by some clear disclaimer; but a responsible critic will want to be his own editor in the last resort. So, too, he must meet the play he studies in the theater, actually and for himself, or else he must acknowledge that he takes certain facts on trust or on secondhand authority, or ignores them altogether. Shakespeare wrote for the theater—that is his medium, the element in which his art is designed to live—and therefore, for all its difficulties, theatrical reality is also *the* element of Shakespeare criticism.

If the theatrical critic of Shakespeare is occupied in discovering possibilities and questions, this should be an accepted condition of much of his work. We should not look for rapid revaluations, or conclude that we have been overemphasizing the basic condition of "stage performance" merely because the object we are viewing seems to change every moment before our very eyes—that is its natural condition. Perhaps the main task of a critic is not to evaluate, fix, place, or penetrate, but to write commentaries that encourage a full engagement with the text in varying conditions of performance; certainly such activity must be a prerequisite for any responsible revaluation.

Besides this basic and exciting work of discovery, other tasks await the theatrical critic. The one that has chiefly engaged me recently is an attempt to outline a "method" for reading a play.[2] I wanted to examine the way I work in the theater

2 See *Shakespeare's Dramatic Style* (forthcoming).

of my mind and, by describing the processes I find most useful,
try to understand one stage in critical awareness more precisely
and so help myself and, hopefully, others to read Shakespeare
with greater consciousness of theatrical potentialities.

Another task is to observe and describe the constants between many productions, and also the theatrical cruxes where
any particular play seems most open to varying realization in
performance. In *The Tempest*, for example, the moment when
Prospero stops the masque is wide open to different interpretations. The character battles with himself in silence, so words
cannot define the struggle. Prospero says that he has

> forgot that foul conspiracy
> Of the beast Caliban and his confederates
> Against my life. The minute of their plot
> Is almost come.—Well done! Avoid! No more!—
>
> (IV.i.139–42)

but he does not say *why* he remembers it now, nor why it is
important, seeing that he is almost godlike in percipience and
controlling power. Why break the dance, in which four elements mingle, just before its completion? Comments on his behavior speak of wonder and alarm, and his own next speech is
addressed to the dismayed onlookers, only indirectly concerned
with himself. In my experience, no two Prosperos have here expressed the same kind of involvement; yet here, clearly, is a
major crux in plot, action, character presentation, thematic development, even in the spectacular impression of the play. Why
did Shakespeare fashion it thus, with only inference as guide?

The critic will all the time relate theatrical possibilities to the text, and seek to judge each effect in the widest context that can be held in his mind. He will find that no speech or gesture has its meaning alone. For example, in *Hamlet*, when Polonius talks of "The best actors in the world, either for tragedy, comedy, history, pastoral . . ." and so forth (II.ii.405 ff.), he has just been outrageously mocked as if he were a "great baby," with Hamlet leading two student-friends (whom he has just learnt not to trust) in a zany attack upon his dignity and good sense. As Polonius calls the prince "My lord," the echo comes back from Hamlet, "My lord," and Polonius replies with yet another "my lord" (but at the sentence end this time): thus repartee is the stuff of this dialogue. It is immediately after this that Polonius launches into his long speech, and the actor may well find psychological justification as well as technical control by stressing the longer rhythms of the new sentence over against the running, thrusting, echoing badinage. After the first long sentence of Polonius' speech, the structure and rhythms then shorten; after an antithesis that is comparatively brisk, the last sentence starts with an adverbial phrase and then a short statement:

For the law of writ and the liberty, these are the only men.

It sounds as if Polonius has won attention by his elaboration and so can bring the speech clearly to a halt. If he has turned away from the mocking and abusive young men, he will be tempted to regain contact with these last words and look them straight in the eyes. Hamlet and his friends may well be silent now, and so Polonius' words "the only men" may thus gain sharp attention and sound like a reproof: these coltish clowns are no men. In performance at this point I have been abruptly reminded of Hamlet's elaborate and careful speech which has just been listened to in silence by Rosencrantz and Guildenstern, the speech about "What a piece of work is a man"; if Polonius gains silence here, his words will seem to touch Hamlet's consciousness at just this point. Something appears to have stirred in his mind, for the prince's next words are rather theatrical, assuming impersonation, but concerned, nevertheless, with judgment, a "fair daughter," and death by sacrifice. *How* Polonius times his speech and speaks the last word in it; *how* the three young men have responded immediately before (are they still laughing?); whether there is a short silence or not; whether Polonius catches Hamlet's eye; *how* Hamlet speaks the following lines: all these elements of the drama in performance are interrelated and together control what the audience sees and hears, and what it understands.

The critic will also look again at the evidence about Elizabethan performances, and use his practical understanding of present-day theater to try to reconstruct the modes of stage realization that are most natural to the text as Shakespeare contrived it. This will involve continual reappraisal, prompted as much by the lack of similarity between today and then as by the similarities. For example, the repertory system of the Elizabethan theaters ensured a particular kind of preparation by the actors. When a play is put on for one night and then dropped for a week, a fortnight, or even several months, some previous rehearsal will be necessary on each occasion. Clearly the timetable of productions in the busy Elizabethan theater season would allow, at the most, one rehearsal onstage; and I do not know any evidence to suggest that they invariably took advantage of this. Each performance of a play under these conditions would have an air of improvisation, of danger, of actors watching carefully for what exactly will happen next, a tone and tension that are entirely absent from our well-drilled, well-oiled productions that run with frequency and often continuously. Elizabethan productions must have been precarious, and must have varied from night to night in over-all effect as well as in incidental force or clarity. If an actor has prepared some words with a large and slow delivery, it would matter very much to him at what pace, pitch, and volume the words immediately before his are spoken: he must respond to their rhythms or else his impressive delivery will sound affected, or ponderous, or funny, or unconvincing. The Elizabethan actor needed a more continuous watchfulness than we can easily imagine, for not only was there little group-rehearsal or developed habit of performance, but he could not possibly gain for himself a precise knowledge of what he was to hear and see; he did not have a copy of the text of the whole play from which to study, only the words of his own "part" and the briefest of verbal cues on which he was due to speak. Elizabethan performances were alert, if not precarious. Whenever Shakespeare was in the audience, or an actor in the play, he must have expected to hear the words he had written in ever-new forms; he must have been used to discovering new possibilities.

A critic who works in the element for which Shakespeare wrote will not always command the assurance which will enable him to argue conclusively for major revaluations of Shakespeare's plays. For much of his time he may well cease to be a critic to become an explorer, a patient collector of questions, possibilities, and potentialities. He will also run the risk of being hooked for life, and he may well spread the habit of never knowing for sure what is *in* Shakespeare's plays waiting to be realized.

I do not think this prospect is disquieting, but what anyone used to theater work would expect. I remember a conversation with T. S. Eliot recorded by Nevil Coghill:

I think I saw you at Rupert Doone's production of *Sweeney Agonistes?* . . . I had no idea the play meant what he made of it . . . that everyone is a Crippen. I was astonished.

So was I.

Then you had meant something very different when you wrote it?

Very different indeed.

Yet you accept Mr. Doone's production?

Certainly.

But . . . but . . . can the play mean something you didn't intend it to mean, you didn't know it meant?

Obviously it does.

But can it then also mean what you *did* intend?

I hope so . . . yes, I think so.

But if the two meanings are contradictory, is not one right and the other wrong? Must not the author be right?

Not necessarily, do you think? Why is either wrong?[3]

[3] *T. S. Eliot: A Symposium,* compiled by Richard March and Tambimuttu (London, 1948), pp. 85–86.

In its theatrical element, a play reveals more of its potentiality all the time, the human implications, the emotional, physical, and intellectual possibilities which belong to its original words, the "meaning" of the whole play. A critic will remain open to these varying realizations by meeting the play in its proper element; and then he will evaluate the play with considerable hesitation.

Beyond this he may speculate. Shakespeare is only a special case, an obvious and superbly complicated example: do we, then, know for sure what is *in* any *play?* Beyond that, do we know what is in any work of art created for us to perceive? The theater may be only the most varying, the least stable, the most endlessly surprising of literary and artistic media; in which case it will be the most accommodating of media, the one most able, in the hands of a master, to speak to any age, through any filter of misunderstanding and inattention—so long as it is perceived in its full and actual theatrical element.

The Program

September 3 Through September 6, 1968

Conferences

I. FREEDOM AND NECESSITY IN LYRIC FORM

Directed by Robert Langbaum, University of Virginia

1. Donne as Bargainer: Freedoms and Necessities in the Elizabethan Dramatic Lyric
   Neil Rudenstine, Princeton University
2. Imitation as Freedom, 1717-1798
   W. K. Wimsatt, Yale University
3. Dynamics of Form and Motive in Some Representative Twentieth-Century Lyrics
   M. L. Rosenthal, New York University

II. BLAKE: "VISIONARY FORMS DRAMATIC"

Directed by David V. Erdman, State University of New York (Stony Brook) and New York Public Library

1. Apprenticeship in the Haymarket?
   Martha Winburn England, Queens College, City University of New York
2. Metamorphoses of a Favorite Cat
   Irene Tayler, Barnard College, Columbia University
3. *America:* New Expanses
   David V. Erdman

III. REINTERPRETATIONS OF ELIZABETHAN DRAMA

Directed by Norman Rabkin, University of California, Berkeley

1. The New Theater and the Old: Reversions and Rejuvenations
   Jonas A. Barish, University of California, Berkeley

2. *Libido Speculandi:* Contemporary Interpretations of Marlowe's *Doctor Faustus*
   Max Bluestone, University of Massachusetts, Boston
3. Shakespeare's Texts and Modern Productions
   Daniel Seltzer, Loeb Drama Center, Harvard University

IV. PRIZE ESSAYS

Directed by Roy Harvey Pearce, University of California, San Diego

1. Shakespeare and the Spectator
   Robert Hapgood, University of New Hampshire
2. Blake's Book of Urizen: The Symmetry of Fear
   Robert E. Simmons, Glendon College, York University
3. The Inevitable Ear: Freedom and Necessity in Lyric Form, Wordsworth and After
   Donald Wesling, University of Essex

Honorable Mention
   Alicia Ostriker, Rutgers University
   W. J. T. Mitchell, The Johns Hopkins University
   H. T. McNeil, Hunter College

Registrants, 1968

Ruth M. Adams, Wellesley College; Flavia M. Alaya, Ridgefield, New Jersey; Gellert S. Alleman, Rutgers University at Newark; George R. Allen, Oxford University Press; Marcia Allentuck, City College, CUNY; Valborg Anderson, Brooklyn College; Sister Ann Edward, Chestnut Hill College; George W. Bahlke, Middlebury College; Stewart A. Baker, Rice University; Jonas Barish, University of California at Berkeley; Rev. J. Robert Barth, s.j., Canisius College; Phyllis Bartlett, Queens College, CUNY; Eben Bass, Geneva College; Rev. John E. Becker, s.j., Rockhurst College; Bernard Benstock, Kent State University; Max Bluestone, University of Massachusetts at Boston; Sister M. Bonaventure, Nazareth College of Rochester; Philip Bordinat, Wright State University; Bro. Francis R. Bowers, f.s.c., Manhattan College; Rev. John D. Boyd, s.j., Fordham University; Frank Brady, City University of New York; Howard S. Bragg III, Atlanta, Georgia; Miriam R. Brokaw, Princeton University Press; Louise Brown, Erskine College; Audrey Brune, Sir George Williams University; James H. Bunn, Emory University; Robert B. Burlin, Bryn Mawr College; George E. Bush, St. Francis College; Grace J. Calder, Hunter College, CUNY; James Van Dyck Card, Old Dominion College; G. H. Carrithers, Jr., State University of New York at Buffalo; Nathan A. Cervo, Hartwick College; Arnold H. Chadderdon, University of Pennsylvania; Leslie F. Chard, University of Cincinnati; Sister Mary Charles, i.h.m., Immaculata College; Hugh C. G. Chase, Bristol, New Hampshire; Kent Christensen, Upsala College; Sister Mary Chrysostom, College of Mount St. Vincent; James L. Clifford, Columbia University; Sister Anne Gertrude Coleman, College of St. Elizabeth; Arthur Nethaway Collins, State University of New York at Albany; Rowland L. Collins, University of Rochester; Ralph W. Condee, Pennsylvania State Univer-

sity; Madeleine Pelnar Cosman, City College, CUNY; David
Cowden, Swarthmore College; Robert P. Creed, State University
of New York at Stony Brook; Curtis Dahl, Wheaton College;
Charles R. Dahlberg, Queens College, CUNY; Marlies K. Dan-
ziger, Hunter College, CUNY; Irene Dash, Columbia University;
Winifred M. Davis, Columbia University; Robert A. Day, Queens
College, CUNY; Charlotte D'Evelyn, Mount Holyoke College
Emeritus; John Dollar, Fairleigh Dickinson University; Mother
Mary Dolores M., Mt. St. Ursula College; John H. Dorenkamp,
Holy Cross College; Victor A. Doyno, State University of New
York at Buffalo; Thomas F. Dunn, Canisius College; David A.
Dushkin, Random House, Inc.; Thomas R. Edwards, Jr., Rutgers
University at New Brunswick; Irvin Ehrenpreis, University of
Virginia; Scott Elledge, Cornell University; George P. Elliott,
Syracuse University; Richard Ellmann, Yale University; Martha
Winburn England, New York, New York; Sister Mary Gonzaga
Erdle, Maria College; David V. Erdman, New York Public Li-
brary; Sister Marie Eugenie, I.H.M., Immaculata College; Doris V.
Falk, Douglass College, Rutgers University; P. D. Fleck, Univer-
sity of Western Ontario; Edward G. Fletcher, University of Texas;
George H. Ford, University of Rochester; Albert Friedman, Clare-
mont Graduate School; Northrop Frye, Victoria College, Univer-
sity of Toronto; Edwin Fussell, University of California at San
Diego; Paul Fussell, Jr., Rutgers University at New Brunswick;
Harry R. Garvin, Bucknell University; Walker Gibson, University
of Massachusetts at Amherst; Donald E. Glover, Mary Washing-
ton College; Anthony Gosse, Bucknell University; Matthew Grace,
City College, CUNY; Thomas J. Grace, Talladega College; Rich-
ard L. Greene, Wesleyan University; Sister M. Jeremins Hall, O.P.,
Siena Heights College; J. B. Halpert, Fairleigh Dickinson Univer-
sity; Robert Halsband, Columbia University; Mrs. William Hanle,
Princeton University Press; Robert Hapgood, University of New
Hampshire; Richard Harrier, New York University; Kathryn
Montgomery Harris, Morehouse College; John A. Hart, Carnegie-
Mellon University; Joan E. Hartman, Queens College, CUNY;
Ann Hayes, Carnegie-Mellon University; Allen T. Hazen, Co-
lumbia University; Elizabeth K. Hill, St. John's University; James

L. Hill, Michigan State University; Rev. William Bernard Hill, s.j., Loyola Seminary; Laurence B. Holland, Princeton University; Frank S. Hook, Lehigh University; Vivian C. Hopkins, State University of New York at Albany; Donald R. Howard, The Johns Hopkins University; J. Paul Hunter, Emory University; Samuel Hynes, Northwestern University; Julia H. Hysham, Skidmore College; Sister Mary Immaculate, c.s.c., Saint Mary's College; Sears Jayne, Hunter College, CUNY; Sister Melinda Keane, Rosemont College; Alfred L. Kellogg, Rutgers University at New Brunswick; Richard S. Kennedy, Temple University; Joseph A. Kinney, Jr., Villanova University; Mary A. Knapp, Albertus Magnus College; Paul J. Korshin, University of Pennsylvania; Joaquin C. Kuhn, Yale University; Lincoln F. Ladd, University of North Carolina at Greensboro; Rev. John P. Lahey, s.j., Le Moyne College; Roy Lamson, Massachusetts Institute of Technology; Robert Langbaum, University of Virginia; Rev. Henry St. Clair Lavin, s.j., University of Scranton; Francis Noel Lees, University of Manchester; George deF. Lord, Yale University; Joseph P. Lovering, Canisius College; Sister Mary Aloyse Lubin, College of St. Elizabeth; Isabel G. MacCaffrey, Bryn Mawr College; Marjorie W. McCune, Susquehanna University; Patricia Ann McFate, University of Illinois at Chicago; Carey McIntosh, Harvard University; Elizabeth T. McLaughlin, Bucknell University; Sister Mary Berchmans Mahoney, Maria College; Donald G. Marshall, Yale University; Mary H. Marshall, Syracuse University; Harold C. Martin, Union College; Louis Martz, Yale University; Donald C. Mell, Jr., University of Delaware; Lore Metzger, Emory University; John H. Middendorf, Columbia University; J. Hillis Miller, The Johns Hopkins University; Sister Jeanne Pierre Mittnight, c.s.j., College of St. Rose; Mother Grace Monahan, o.s.u., College of New Rochelle; William T. Moynihan, University of Connecticut; Lowry Nelson, Jr., Yale University; Rev. William T. Noon, s.j., Le Moyne College; Sister M. Norma, Albertus Magnus College; Paul E. O'Connell, Prentice-Hall, Inc.; Eileen O'Gorman, r.s.c.j., Manhattanville College; Rev. Joseph E. O'Neill, s.j., Fordham University; Mother Thomas Aquinas O'Reilly, o.s.u., College of New Rochelle; Carol Orr, Princeton University Press; James M. Osborn, New

Haven, Connecticut; Charles A. Owen, Jr., University of Connecticut; Harry Pauley, Shippensburg (Pa.) State College; Roy Harvey Pearce, University of California at San Diego; Norman Holmes Pearson, Yale University; Harry William Pedicord, Thiel College; Marjorie Perloff, Catholic University; Oliver L. Peters, University of Wyoming; Henry H. Peyton III, Memphis State University; Barry Phillips, Wellesley College; Anne Lake Prescott, Barnard College, Columbia University; Robert O. Preyer, Brandeis University; Richard E. Quaintance, Jr., Douglass College, Rutgers University; Norman Rabkin, University of California at Berkeley; Virginia L. Radley, Russell Sage College; Paul Ramsey, University of Chattanooga; Donald H. Reiman, The Carl H. Pforzheimer Library; Sister Rita Margaret, o.p., Caldwell College for Women; Roger B. Rollin, Franklin and Marshall College; Edward J. Rose, University of Alberta; Shirley Rose, University of Alberta; Sister Rose Bernard Donna, c.s.j., College of St. Rose; M. L. Rosenthal, New York University; Neil Rudenstine, Princeton University; Richard Ruland, Washington University at St. Louis; Edwin St. Vincent, Randolph-Macon Woman's College; Irene Samuel, Hunter College, CUNY; Bernard N. Schilling, University of Rochester; Helene B. M. Schnabel, New York, New York; Daniel Seltzer, Loeb Drama Center, Harvard University; Richard Sexton, Fordham University; Michael Shapiro, University of Illinois at Urbana; F. Parvin Sharpless, Germantown Friends School; Catherine M. Shaw, University of Illinois at Chicago; John T. Shawcross, University of Wisconsin; James D. Simmons, University of Pittsburgh; Calvin Skaggs, Drew University; Carol H. Smith, Douglass College, Rutgers University; Patricia Adel Smith, Yale University; Rowland Smith, Dalhousie University; Nelle Smither, Douglass College, Rutgers University; George Soule, Carleton College; Ian Sowton, University of Alberta; J. Gordon Spaulding, University of British Columbia; Hugh Sproule, Dalhousie University; Susan Staves, Brandeis University; Donald R. Stoddard, Skidmore College; Maureen T. Sullivan, University of Pennsylvania; Joseph H. Summers, Michigan State University; Donald R. Swanson, Upsala College; Irene Tayler, Barnard College, Columbia University; Anne Robb Taylor, Skidmore College; Peter A. Taylor, University of British

Columbia; Sister Loretta Mary Tenbusch, I.H.M., Marygrove College; Charles B. Teske, Oberlin College; Sister Thomas Marion, Nazareth College of Rochester; A. Robert Towers, Jr., Queens College, CUNY; Donald Tritschler, Skidmore College; Margret G. Trotter, Agnes Scott College; Mary Curtis Tucker, Marietta, Georgia; John Unterecker, Columbia University; Thomas Vance, Dartmouth College; Sister M. Vincentia, O.P., Albertus Magnus College; Sister M. Vivian, O.P., Caldwell College for Women; E. M. Waith, Yale University; A. J. Walker, Georgia Institute of Technology; Carey Wall, University of California at Los Angeles; Aileen Ward, Brandeis University; Sister Mary Anthony Weinig, Rosemont College; Edward R. Weismiller, Pomona College; Jeanne K. Welcher, C. W. Post College; Sister Julia Marie Weser, College of Mount St. Vincent; George Wickes, Harvey Mudd College; Joseph Wiesenfarth, F.S.C., Manhattan College; Elizabeth Wiley, Susquehanna University; M. Denise Wilkens, King's College; Lyle Givens Williams, University of Southwestern Louisiana; Sister Margaret Williams, R.S.C.J., Manhattanville College; Dorothy M. Willis, New Haven, Connecticut; W. K. Wimsatt, Yale University; Eleanor Withington, Queens College, CUNY; Carl Woodring, Columbia University; Steven A. Zemelman, Amherst College.